STENDHAL

EDITED AND WITH AN
INTRODUCTION BY HAROLD BLOOM

BLOOM'S MAJOR DRAMATISTS

Aeschylus

Anton Chekhov

Aristophanes

Berthold Brecht

Euripides

Henrik Ibsen

Ben Johnson

Christopher
  Marlowe

Arthur Miller

Eugene O'Neill

Shakespeare's
  Comedies

Shakespeare's
  Histories

Shakespeare's
  Romances

Shakespeare's
  Tragedies

George Bernard
  Shaw

Neil Simon

Sophocles

Tennessee
  Williams

August Wilson

BLOOM'S MAJOR NOVELISTS

Jane Austen

The Brontës

Willa Cather

Stephen Crane

Charles Dickens

Fyodor Dostoevsky

William Faulkner

F. Scott Fitzgerald

Thomas Hardy

Nathaniel Hawthorne

Ernest Hemingway

Henry James

James Joyce

D. H. Lawrence

Toni Morrison

John Steinbeck

Stendhal

Leo Tolstoy

Mark Twain

Alice Walker

Edith Wharton

Virginia Woolf

BLOOM'S MAJOR WORLD POETS

Geoffrey Chaucer

Emily Dickinson

John Donne

T. S. Eliot

Robert Frost

Langston Hughes

John Milton

Edgar Allan Poe

Shakespeare's Poems
  & Sonnets

Alfred, Lord
  Tennyson

Walt Whitman

William Wordsworth

BLOOM'S MAJOR SHORT STORY WRITERS

William Faulkner

F. Scott Fitzgerald

Ernest Hemingway

O. Henry

James Joyce

Herman Melville

Flannery O'Connor

Edgar Allan Poe

J. D. Salinger

John Steinbeck

Mark Twain

Eudora Welty

STENDHAL

COMPREHENSIVE RESEARCH
AND STUDY GUIDE

BLOOM'S

MAJOR
NOVELISTS

EDITED AND WITH AN INTRODUCTION
BY HAROLD BLOOM

First Printing
1 3 5 7 9 8 6 4 2

Library of Congress Cataloging-in-Publication Data
Stendhal / edited and with an introduction by Harold Bloom.
    p. cm.— (Bloom's major novelists)
    Includes bibliographical references and index.
    ISBN 0-7910-6351-8 (alk. paper)
  1. Stendhal, 1783–1842—Examinations—Study guides. 2. Stendhal,
  1783-1842—Criticism and interpretation.   I. Bloom, Harold.   II. Series.

PQ2441 .S69 2001
843'.7—dc21   2001047495

Chelsea House Publishers
1974 Sproul Road, Suite 400
Broomall, PA 19008-0914

The Chelsea House World Wide Web address is
http://www.chelseahouse.com

Series Editor: Matt Uhler

Contributing Editor: Jesse Zuba

Produced by Publisher's Services, Santa Barbara, California

Contents

User's Guide

This volume is designed to present biographical, critical, and bibliographical information on the author's best-known or most important works. Following Harold Bloom's editor's note and introduction is a detailed biography of the author, discussing major life events and important literary accomplishments. A plot summary of each novel follows, tracing significant themes, patterns, and motifs in the work.

A selection of critical extracts, derived from previously published material from leading critics, analyzes aspects of each work. The extracts consist of statements from the author, if available, early reviews of the work, and later evaluations up to the present. A bibliography of the author's writings (including a complete list of all works written, cowritten, edited, and translated), a list of additional books and articles on the author and his or her work, and an index of themes and ideas in the author's writings conclude the volume.

~

Harold Bloom is Sterling Professor of the Humanities at Yale University and Henry W. and Albert A. Berg Professor of English at the New York University Graduate School. He is the author of over 20 books, including *Shelley's Mythmaking* (1959), *The Visionary Company* (1961), *Blake's Apocalypse* (1963), *Yeats* (1970), *A Map of Misreading* (1975), *Kabbalah and Criticism* (1975), *Agon: Toward a Theory of Revisionism* (1982), *The American Religion* (1992), *The Western Canon* (1994), and *Omens of Millennium: The Gnosis of Angels, Dreams, and Resurrection* (1996). *The Anxiety of Influence* (1973) sets forth Professor Bloom's provocative theory of the literary relationships between the great writers and their predecessors. His most recent books include *Shakespeare: The Invention of the Human,* a 1998 National Book Award finalist, and *How to Read and Why,* which was published in 2000.

Professor Bloom earned his Ph.D. from Yale University in 1955 and has served on the Yale faculty since then. He is a 1985 MacArthur Foundation Award recipient, served as the Charles Eliot Norton Professor of Poetry at Harvard University in 1987–88, and has received honorary degrees from the universities of Rome and Bologna. In 1999, Professor Bloom received the prestigious American Academy of Arts and Letters Gold Medal for Criticism.

Currently, Harold Bloom is the editor of numerous Chelsea House volumes of literary criticism, including the series BLOOM'S NOTES, BLOOM'S MAJOR DRAMATISTS, BLOOM'S MAJOR NOVELISTS, MAJOR LITERARY CHARACTERS, MODERN CRITICAL VIEWS, MODERN CRITICAL INTERPRETATIONS, and WOMEN WRITERS OF ENGLISH AND THEIR WORKS.

Editor's Note

My Introduction contrasts the erotic stances of *The Red and the Black* and *The Charterhouse of Parma.*

Stendhal himself leads off the critical views of *The Red and the Black,* with a projected self-review, in which he memorably remarks that the Parisian woman loves her lover only to the extent *that each morning she believes herself to be on the point of losing him.*

Erich Auerbach relates Stendhal's mode of realistic representation to his freedom from a romanticized historicism, like that of Sir Walter Scott, after which the Prince of Lampedusa, author of the superb novel, *The Leopard,* defends Julien's energetic amorality, and commends Stendhal for "honesty of genius" in killing Julien so as to be free of him.

The Stendhal scholar Henri Martineau regards Julien's attempt to murder Madame de Rênal as a crime of passion, while the feminist Simone de Beauvoir finds in her a generous heart, ready to be set ablaze.

The scholar George Blin ascribes a kind of *rapid* realism to Stendhal, after which the critic Irving Howe characterizes Julien as an odd blend of Byron and Marx.

Stendhal's fondness for ambiguity is cited by Robert M. Adams as the reason why we are left uncertain as to Julien's parentage, while Harry Levin shrewdly remarks that Julien's hypocrisy, like Hamlet's madness, is a dramatic stratagem.

To Victor Brombert, what charms us about Julien is his blindness as to his own emotions, after which Michael Wood also describes the hero as knowing nothing about himself.

D. A. Miller subtly suggests that Julien's true motive in trying to slay Madame de Rênal was to restore her centrality for him, while Peter Brooks, also very subtly, indicates how *The Red and the Black* perpetually subverts the authority of all father-figures.

Margaret Mauldon rather wonderfully describes Julien's story as "a catalogue of miscommunications," after which Christopher Prendergast emphasizes that Julien's conquest of society depends upon mastering social codes of speech.

The great Balzac reviews *The Charterhouse of Parma,* and acclaims it as the Sublime, upon the heights of novelistic art, while the critic Emile Faguet, writing in 1892, prefers Julien to Fabrizio, because Julien is energetic and the later hero mostly passive.

George Lukács, eminent Marxist critic, rather weirdly sees Romanticism as a rebellion against Capitalism, and then presents us with a Stendhal who is anti-Romantic, which would have greatly surprised Stendhal himself.

In the judgment of Jean-Pierre Richard, Stendhal and his heroes are Adamic figures, which to me makes sense in regard to Fabrizio, but not at all when we consider Stendhal and his Julien.

Fabrizio's metamorphosis during his imprisonment is described by Robert M. Adams as an allegory or ironic version of Stendhal's own development into an artist of subversion, after which Jean Starobinski introduces his irony of a Stendhal imprisoned in his own body, neither young nor beautiful.

The rhetoricism Gérard Genette sees all of Stendhal's fiction as a unity, while Victor Brombert delightfully exposes the mock-heroic element in Fabrizio's experiences of the Battle of Waterloo.

For Leo Bersani, society plays a double role in Stendhal's visions of happiness, both saving it from self-imprisonment but also confirming such a tendency.

Michael Wood reads the *Charterhouse* as a "tired romance," after which Stendhal's theme of incest is explored by Alison Finch and Roland Barthes celebrates Stendhal's liberation from "speechlessness" by the formal demands of novelistic composition.

The poet-translator Richard Howard splendidly commends Stendhal for his elliptical qualities, while Harold Bloom speculates upon the influences of Shakespeare and Cervantes upon *The Charterhouse of Parma.*

Introduction

HAROLD BLOOM

When I was younger, even in my middle years, I greatly preferred *The Red and the Black* to *The Charterhouse of Parma*. In old age, I have experienced a reversal. I still reread each novel every year or so, but I am more consistently delighted by the *Charterhouse*. Both books are ironic masterpieces, but the cold splendor of the story of Julien Sorel does not charm me as much as the more nostalgic saga of the Duchess Sanseverina, surely one of the most desirable women in all of literature. One doesn't feel that Stendhal is in love with Mathilde or with Madame de Rênal, but his passion for the Sanseverina is palpable.

After Shakespeare, who strongly influenced him, Stendhal is one of the Western authors who best teaches us what we need to know about the illusions and the realities of sexual love. It is difficult to withstand the Stendhalian analysis that divides "being in love" into equal components of gratified vanity and pathology. Our resistance to this analysis, particularly when we are in such a state, can be intense, but the ironic truths of Stendhal have the auras of reality.

Stendhal himself lost his mother at seven, and missed her all his life, while hating his father cordially. Loyal to Napoleon, Stendhal was a trusted functionary in the War Ministry until his emperor's defeat. His passion for Angela Pietragrua informs his portrait of the Sanseverina, Gina Pietranera, while his difficult courtship of a woman named Mathilde may have prompted his comic vision of Mathilde in *The Red and the Black*. Dead at fifty-nine, Stendhal was aware that he was ahead of his time, but has now enjoyed consistent fame and a huge audience for the last one hundred and twenty years. Energetic as he is, he cannot match Balzac and Victor Hugo, preternatural demiurges of creativity, and his art is precisely the reverse of Flaubert's painstaking mastery. André Gide preferred *The Charterhouse of Parma* to every other French novel, but then Gide rejected for publication *Swann's Way*, the first volume of Proust's *In Search of Lost Time*, certainly the masterwork of all French fiction.

Despite the many similarities between *The Red and the Black* and *The Charterhouse of Parma*, they are subtly different in their erotic stances, and in their representation of Stendhal's protagonists. The nostalgia for Napoleonic glory does not abandon Julien until almost the end, but dies in Fabrizio after his fiasco at Waterloo. Authentic love does not possess Julien until his final days, and while his sincerity need not then be doubted, both he and Madame de Rênal know that they have no future, a considerable incitement premium for heightening passion.

In *The Charterhouse of Parma,* no man can contemplate Gina without desiring her, except for Fabrizio, fearful of the incest barrier, which does not restrain the Duchess, who cares only for him. Fabrizio's final passion, for Clélia, is as definitive as Gina's for him. And yet Stendhal is the least monumental of novelists (short of Ronald Firbank!), and so we, his happy readers (no longer few) never altogether believe in these transcendent loves. It is not this improbable erotic stance that makes me prefer *The Charterhouse of Parma* to the more realistic and Stendhalian eros of *The Red and the Black.* Rather, the improvisatory verve of the *Charterhouse* sweeps me away. Its translator, Richard Howard, makes the marvelous point that you must reread the novel even as you read it, because nearly everyone who matters in it reinvents himself or herself incessantly, a Shakespearean element in Stendhal. Again as in Shakespeare (and in life), no one in Stendhal ever really listens to what anyone else is saying, particularly if they regard themselves as being in love with the speaker. Though Stendhal knew Italy well, his Italy, like Shakespeare's, is a romantic country of the mind. *The Red and the Black's* Paris, and even its fictive Verrières, inspire Stendhal to a cold erotic realism, whereas his Italy of the mind allows him to yield to visions of a more extravagant eros. Stendhal's Parma could be the Verona of *Romeo and Juliet,* whereas *The Red and the Black* prophesies the erotic universe of Proust's *In Search of Lost Time,* where jealousy over-determines every sexual attachment.

Paul Valéry phrased it best about Stendhal: "He makes the reader proud to be his reader." That means that we forgive his protagonists *everything*. Julien Sorel has no self-knowledge, feels passions only after simulating them, and has a genius for hypocrisy. And yet Julien more than retains our interest: he fascinates us, and we cannot dislike him. Everyone in Stendhal is selfish, but then so are we.

In the *Charterhouse,* Mosca, the coolest head in Stendhal, always sets his own happiness first. The magnificent Gina has the vivacity of a Shakespearean heroine, a Rosalind or a Beatrice, but she plots a murder, gives herself to the younger Prince of Parma as a one-time payment, and generally confounds all our expectations. We love her the more for it.

The secret of Stendhal may be that he conceived of life as a novel, but did not confuse the novel with life. He improvises because he knows that he is not Shakespeare; he cannot write as life does. Who, besides Shakespeare, could? Dante, Chaucer, Cervantes, Homer, the Bible, and—post-Stendhal—Tolstoy, Proust, Joyce. Stendhal would not pretend to be of that visionary company, but he did not need to be. ❀

Biography of
Stendhal

Marie Henri Beyle, later known as Stendhal, was born into a respectable middle-class family in Grenoble, France in 1783, six years before increasing political turbulence would culminate in the Revolution and the rise of the Napoleonic Empire. His autobiographical *Life of Henri Brulard* documents his intense affection for his mother, who died when he was seven and for whom he cherished a love proportionate to the hatred he bore his father, a business-minded reactionary. Beyle's rebellion against his father amplified his own liberal leanings, though he retained a passionate admiration for the aristocracy and the ancien régime throughout his life. He attended the Ecole Centrale in Grenoble, excelling at art and math and developing a background in logic and the sciences before leaving for Paris in 1799. Abandoning his plans for continuing his education, he secured a position in Napoleon's War Ministry, but left shortly thereafter to join the army, which sent him to Milan. He returned to Paris after just one year abroad and resigned from the army in order to pursue a career as a playwright. His early literary endeavors proved futile, and in 1806 he rejoined the War Ministry and climbed quickly in the imperial bureaucracy, following his job to Germany, Italy, and Russia, where he witnessed Napoleon's defeat at Moscow in 1812.

Beyle's return to Milan after the fall of Napoleon was likely motivated by his romantic involvement with Angela Pietragrua, the first of the mistresses in his notoriously crowded love-life to be carried over into his writings—as Gina Pietranera in *The Charterhouse of Parma*. Pietragrua was succeeded by Mathilde Viscontini-Dembowska, whose unstinting resistance to Beyle lasted for six years and inspired the self-analysis and confessions of *On Love*, which sold only seventeen copies but nevertheless stands as his first great work. Before *On Love* he had published the two-volume *History of Painting in Italy and Rome, Naples, and Florence*, both of which appeared in 1817. The mild success of the latter, which he wrote as "M. de Stendhal," led to his regular adoption of the pseudonym he was to make famous.

Beyle used over 150 pseudonyms over the course of his career, and his taste for variety also registers in his habit of frequent relocation—he rarely stayed at one address for more than half a year—and in the generic diversity of his oeuvre, which compasses journalism, poetry, criticism, political commentaries, short fiction, biography, and novels, among much else. Under political pressure to leave Milan, he returned to Paris in 1821 and published *Racine and Shakespeare,* a manifesto for romanticism in which he celebrates the psychological complexities of Shakespeare and argues for the relative nature of beauty. Free of his agonizing attachment to Mathilde, Beyle began a tumultuous affair with the Countess Clementine Curial that ended in 1826, one year before he managed to publish *Armance,* his first novel, at the age of forty-four. As commercially unsuccessful as most of his literary endeavors, *Armance* takes up the theme of personal happiness that runs through much of his later works, and examines with Beyle's signature perspicuity the psychology of Octave, the novel's impotent hero, who commits suicide rather than yield to the conventions of society. He published his *Roman Journal,* a collection of travel sketches based on materials from his early notebooks two years later.

On the night of October 25, 1829 Beyle experienced the "idea of Julien" and drafted a preliminary version of *The Red and the Black* within a few months. Based in part on an account of the criminal career of Antoine Berthet, whose exploits roughly parallel those of Julien Sorel, *The Red and the Black* brings together in one place the abilities and ideas that Beyle's previous books had provided only isolated glimpses of. Like *Armance,* it pits a sensitive protagonist against a problematic society and explores the mind of its hero with near-clinical rigor. The author claimed to have derived his style in the narrative by reading the *Code Napoleon* on a daily basis, an influence reflected in the novel's clipped tone and irregular cadences. Probably Beyle's most famous work, it nevertheless failed to make much of a stir in its own day.

After *The Red and the Black* appeared in 1830, Beyle focused almost entirely on fiction and autobiography. He moved back to Italy, where he served as Consul in Civita-Vecchia from 1831 to 1836. During this period he worked on *The Life of Henri Brulard* and *Souvenirs of Egotism,* both of which were published posthumously, in 1890 and 1892 respectively. Both works are autobiographical: the former chronicles the first seventeen years of his life, concluding with his enrollment in Napoleon's army in 1800; the latter follows his activities during the 1820s. Beyle also attempted a third novel, *Lucien Leuwen,* which he left unfinished. Like its predecessors, *Lucien Leuwen* opposes its hero to his society and chronicles a quest for identity and happiness, though Lucien, unlike Octave and Julien, is not prey to a marked sense of cultural alienation. A classic-in-the-making, *Lucien Leuwen* appeared posthumously in 1894.

During the late 1830s Beyle worked on his biography of Napoleon and published a travelogue entitled *Memoirs of a Tourist* (1838). He also continued to work on a series of short stories that appeared in journals and reviews and were published posthumously as the *Italian Chronicles.* Working at the height of inspiration, he produced his second and last masterpiece, *The Charterhouse of Parma,* in just over seven weeks in 1838. Composed by dictation as the author's health steadily worsened, *The Charterhouse of Parma* is an achievement on par with *The Red and the Black,* and it received an admiring review from Balzac when it was published. Inspired by a quasi-historical Renaissance account of Alexandre Farnese, the novel boldly mixes the conventions of the political satire, the mock-epic military chronicle, and the romance, as it tracks Fabrizio del Dongo through heroic exploits and amorous intrigues to his melancholic withdrawal into the Charterhouse of the novel's title.

Beyle died on March 23, 1842 following a series of strokes and was buried on the 24th in the cemetery of Montmartre. He once predicted that he would not be famous until 1880, and his prediction was to prove uncannily accurate, as growing interest in his work provoked the posthumous appearance of a number of previously unpublished books, including *A Life of Napoleon* (1876), *Journal of Stendhal* (1888) and *Lamiel* (1889). His reputation continued to grow following the turn of the century: André Gide pronounced *The Charterhouse of Parma* the greatest French novel of all time in 1913, and Erich Auerbach named him the co-founder (with Balzac) of modern realism in his famous study *Mimesis,* which appeared in 1946. The continuing attention accorded his work confirms the high praise of Paul Valéry, who declared we should "never be finished with Stendhal." ❈

Plot Summary of
The Red and the Black

The broad outline of Julien Sorel's career parallels that of Antoine Berthet, whose story Stendhal would have read, about a year before his idea for the protagonist of *The Red and the Black* crystallized, in *La Gazette des Tribuneaux,* a newspaper devoted to notable legal trials of the day. The son of a tradesman, Berthet served as a tutor to the children of a local official with whose wife he later became romantically involved. He then entered the seminary, which he left to take a position as an instructor in another household, this time seducing his employer's daughter before being dismissed. Still in love with his first mistress but upset by suspicions of her infidelity, Berthet followed her to church and shot her during the service. Stendhal uses Berthet's scandalous story to contextualize an interrogation of the boundary between history and the novel, and as a way of structuring explorations of the political, moral, psychological, and aesthetic themes elaborated in *The Red and the Black.*

The novel is set in Verrières, a fictional mountain village in eastern France, in 1830, over a decade after the ousting of Napoleon and the restoration of the Bourbons to the throne—an event that divides the country (and Verrières) into the two camps represented by the colors in the novel's title: red is associated with the army and liberals sympathetic to the empire, black with the clergy and royalists sympathetic to the monarchy. As the novel opens, M. de Rênal, mayor of Verrières, decides to hire Julien Sorel, the talented son of a local sawyer, to tutor his children. Julien's father is only too glad to be rid of his son, whom he regards as a bookish good-for-nothing, though old Sorel shrewdly secures a good salary for him in his negotiations with Rênal.

Julien proves himself a worthwhile investment. He is capable of reciting at length from the Bible in Latin, and he gets along well with the Rênal children, whose admiration for him does much to increase his appeal in the eyes of Mme. de Rênal. One of the maids makes advances toward Julien, but he rejects her, and the episode prompts a telling joy in Mme. de Rênal, whose naiveté protects her from recognizing her scandalous feelings for what they are. Having caught on to Mme. de Rênal's budding interest in him, Julien resolves to seduce her, in large part as a way of showing his contempt for M. de Rênal.

He succeeds, but his success results from the boyish charm that Mme. de Rênal sees in his displays of awkwardness rather than the efficacy of his strategies.

Their affair begins in earnest, in spite of the taint of ambition that marks Julien's feelings and the pious devotion that complicates those of Mme. de Rênal. She helps him to polish his manners and fills him in on local political intrigues. When Charles X visits Verrières, she manages to get Julien a prestigious place in the guard of honor. Their relationship goes smoothly until M. de Rênal receives an anonymous letter exposing them. Mme. de Rênal devises a plan to throw her husband off their trail: she leads him to believe that the anonymous message is a falsehood concocted out of jealousy by M. Valenod, his rival. She also recommends that Julien be sent away until the scandal blows over. M. de Rênal buys her story without too much ado: it permits him to gloat over Valenod and to avoid endangering his comfortable situation by probing into the matter.

Elisa, Mme. de Rênal's maid, confesses to Chélan her knowledge of Julien's involvement with Mme. de Rênal, and the priest orders him to enroll in the seminary at Besançon, which is directed by Chélan's friend Pirard. After a final rendezvous with Mme. de Rênal, Julien departs for the seminary. His excellence alienates him from his classmates, but he makes a positive impression on Pirard, and the Marquis de la Mole, an influential aristocrat whom Pirard has assisted in a lawsuit, anonymously bestows a sum of money on Julien. Under pressure to leave the seminary, Pirard obtains a position at the head of a parish in Paris through the generosity of the marquis, also securing a secretarial position for Julien in M. de la Mole's household. Book I ends as Julien flees Verrières after paying a final visit to Mme. de Rênal.

Julien makes himself valuable to the marquis, despite his lack of urbanity and grace. Struck by his scorn for the superficialities of high society, the marquis's haughty daughter Mathilde takes an interest in Julien. He devotes himself assiduously to the marquis, whose business he dispatches with efficiency and intelligence, and whom he learns to look on as a father, even as the marquis eventually regards Julien as a son.

Following his return from a business trip to England, Mathilde invites Julien to a ball. She is the center of attention at the event, though Julien, deep in conversation with Altamira, an aristocratic

Italian idealist, remains uninterested in her. Piqued by his indifference and the loftiness of spirit that his admiration for Altamira evinces, Mathilde falls in love with Julien, associating him with her heroic ancestor Boniface de la Mole, whose beheading foreshadows that of the protagonist. He notes her increasing attention to him, but his fears of being duped or embarrassed cause him to second-guess his impressions. Having caught on to the way his indifference seems to incite her affection, Julien makes a pretense of leaving on business to test her; she responds by avowing her love to him. The courtship turns comedic as Julien, still burdened by distrust, sends a copy of her letter to Fouqué as a precaution against any trickery. He agrees to a rendezvous with Mathilde, but the two consummate their relationship only after Julien overcomes an attack of paranoia that leads him to check under her bed for accomplices upon arriving.

Julien finds he loves Mathilde, and he is agonized by the coolness she shows him following their meeting. Maintaining her favor proves an exercise in hypocrisy: she loves him only when he pretends to feel indifferent toward her. Called upon to deliver a secret message for a group of aristocrats, Julien meets his friend Korasoff, who advises Julien to regain Mathilde by sparking her jealousy. Back in Paris, Julien pretends to court the prudish Mme. de Fervaques using a set of love letters Korasoff gave him—an episode that crowns the novel's complex treatment of epistolary conventions. Julien regains Mathilde, but not without realizing that keeping her means keeping up his pretense of detachment.

Mathilde reveals she is pregnant, and the news dashes the marquis's hopes for his daughter and sends him into a rage. Convinced of Mathilde's devotion to her lover, M. de la Mole provides the couple with money and obtains a position in the army for Julien. Inquiring into his personal history, he learns from Mme. de Rênal of Julien's reputation as an opportunist and a seducer of wealthy women. Mathilde writes to Julien in Strasbourg to let him know that all is lost. Upon learning the news Julien journeys to Verrières and shoots Mme. de Rênal in church.

Julien awaits his trial in prison, and Mathilde and Fouqué develop schemes for securing his acquittal. He receives a number of visits, in spite of his desire for solitude and resignation to his fate. He realizes that he still loves Mme. de Rênal, who miraculously survives his attempt on her life. Sentenced to the guillotine despite Mathilde's efforts to influence the jury, Julien finds peace through his reunion with Mme. de Rênal, who visits him in prison. Following Julien's execution, Mathilde steals his severed head and buries it herself, thus reenacting Queen Margarite's theft and burial of the head of Boniface de la Mole. Mme. de Rênal dies shortly after, and Fouqué sees to it that Julien's remains are buried in accordance with his wishes, on a hill outside of Verrières. ❁

List of Characters in
The Red and the Black

Julien Sorel is the intelligent, proud, and ambitious hero of the novel, which chronicles his career from the provinces to Paris to prison. The protégé of an old army surgeon who impresses him with a yearning for glory, Julien's bookishness, slender build, and pale complexion belie his demonic drive: he would "die a thousand deaths rather than fail to make his fortune." His humble origins combine with his instinctive sense of nobility to produce a strong class-hatred, and he is quick to take umbrage from his superiors. Though much given to self-reflection and calculation, his seductions of Louise de Rênal and Mathilde de la Mole succeed in spite of his schemes rather than because of them, and his romantic involvements point up opposing aspects of his character: Mme. de Rênal loves him for the childish quality and humane sensitivity that show through his poor manners, while Mathilde loves him for his histrionic rebelliousness and talent for hypocrisy. Sentenced to the guillotine, he finds a measure of happiness in rediscovering his love for Mme. de Rênal, with whom he is reunited in prison following his unsuccessful attempt to murder her.

Mme. de Rênal, the wife of the mayor of Verrières, is gifted with the "beauty of the countryside" and an "innocence and liveliness" that permit her to fall in love with her children's tutor before becoming enough aware of the development to resist it. As Simone de Beauvoir observes, "she has preserved a generous heart, capable of violent emotions, and she has a flair for happiness"—qualities that set her apart from the money-grubbers and petty intriguers that surround her. Her simple elegance and maternal tenderness represent contrasts to Mathilde's snobbish urbanity and daughterly sense of entitlement. Devoted to Julien in spite of her ethical and religious scruples, she forgives him his attempt on her life and keeps him company during his time in prison. She dies three days after her lover "in the act of embracing her children."

Mathilde de la Mole, Julien's second mistress, is the clever, haughty, and idealistic daughter of the Marquis de la Mole, Julien's aristocratic benefactor. She is in many ways a female version of Julien, whose self-centeredness, pride, and contempt for high social decorum she shares, as well as his literary bent, his imagination, and his nostalgia for past heroic ages. The "most envied heiress of the Faubourg Saint Germaine," she nevertheless falls for her father's secretary largely because of the indifference he displays toward her, and she evinces a mechanical susceptibility to such displays as their relationship progresses: only when she is confident of Julien's affections does she despise him—a perverse emotional economy that turns their courtship into a "grotesque comedy of arrogance and counter-arrogance," as Robert Adams observes. Passionate guardian of the memory of her ancestor Boniface de la Mole, she reenacts Marguerite de Navarre's part in his illustrious history by stealing and burying Julien's head following his execution at the guillotine.

M. de Rênal, the royalist mayor of Verrières, hires Julien as a tutor for his children in order to uphold his rank among the townspeople. An unsympathetic foil to Julien, M. de Rênal possesses an "air of self-satisfaction, perhaps of sufficiency, combined with something limited and unimaginative" that would strike the reader, the narrator insinuates, on first glance. He is vain and possesses no strength of character—a trait elucidated by his convenient defection to the liberals later in the novel, as well as the cowardly indecisiveness and self-important bluster with which he responds to news of his wife's adultery.

The **Marquis de la Mole**, a wealthy and influential Paris aristocrat, brings Julien to the city to serve as his secretary, and although initially disappointed with Julien's poor manners, the marquis learns to appreciate his unaffectedness and intelligence—an appreciation that develops into a fatherly regard. Like the rest of the aristocratic personages in the novel, the marquis is profoundly world-weary and proud, though his respect for Julien, exemplified in his decision to press him into the service of the ring of royalist conspirators, makes him more sympathetic than M. de Rênal and Old Sorel among the father-figures the novel provides for Julien. His hopes for Julien, whose natural nobility he seeks to legitimatize by awarding him the Legion of Honor and by promoting rumors of his aristocratic birth, survive even the news of his daughter's scandalous relationship with him, but are dashed by Mme. de Rênal's report of Julien as a rakish opportunist. ❀

Critical Views on
The Red and the Black

[Stendhal (1783–1842) drafted a review of *The Red and the Black* in 1832, about a year after the novel was published. The following extract, drawn from Stendhal's review, brings to light his concerns with addressing both urban and provincial readerships, with the novel's contemporary setting, and with the perspectives on romance and morality the novel represents.]

The 'petites bourgeoises' of the provinces ask only of the author that he provide them with extraordinary scenes sufficient to reduce them to floods of tears; *little does it matter how* he devises such scenes. The ladies of Paris, on the other hand, as consumers of octavo novels, take a devilishly severe view of *extra-ordinary* episodes. The moment an event appears to have been introduced into the plot at a particular point merely to show the hero off to advantage, they put the book down and proceed to regard the author as nothing but a figure of fun.

It is because of these two *opposite requirements* that it is so difficult to write a novel which will be read both in the sitting-rooms of the provincial bourgeoise and in the drawing-rooms of Paris.

This was how the novel stood with the French reading public of 1830. The genius of Walter Scott had made the Middle Ages fashionable, and one was sure of success if one spent two pages describing the view from the hero's room, two more pages describing his manner of dress, and a further two depicting the chair on which he sat. M. de S., bored with all this medievalism, all this talk of ogive arches and fifteenth-century costume, dared recount an adventure which took place in 1830 and yet leave the reader totally in the dark as to the type of dresses worn by Mme de Rênal and Mlle de la Mole, his two heroines (for two heroines this novel has, against all the previous rules of the genre).

The author has dared much more than this; he has dared to depict the character of the Parisian woman who loves her lover only to the degree *that each morning she believes herself to be on the point of losing him.*

Such is the result of the immense vanity which has become almost the only identifiable passion in this city of clever people. Elsewhere a lover can ensure that he is loved by protesting the ardour of his passion, his faithfulness, etc., etc., and by showing his fair lady these laudable qualities in action. In Paris, the more he convinces her that his affections will never alter, that he *adores* her, the more he ruins his chances in the mind of his beloved. This is something the Germans will never understand, but I am much afraid that M. de S. has provided an accurate portrait. [. . .]

People abroad are quite ignorant of French *moral attitudes,* which is why it has been necessary to point out before dealing specifically with M. de S.'s novel that nowhere could be less like the gay, amusing, rather libertine France which set the tone throughout Europe from 1715 to 1789 than the earnest, moral, morose France we have been left with by the Jesuits, the **congrégations**, and the Bourbons who ruled between 1814 and 1830. As nothing is more difficult in novels than to paint what one sees and not to *copy from books,* no one before M. de S. had yet attempted to portray these forms of behaviour, unappealing as they are but which nevertheless, thanks to the sheeplike mentality of Europe, will end up being the norm from Naples to Saint-Petersburg.

—Stendhal, "Projet d'un Article sur *Le Rouge et le Noir*," *Le Rouge et le Noir,* ed. Pierre-Georges Castex (Paris: Garnier frères, 1973). Reprinted in *Stendhal,* ed. Roger Pearson (London: Longman, 1994): pp. 31–32.

DEVELOPMENT OF REALISM

[Erich Auerbach (1892–1957) taught at Marburg University and the Turkish State University before immigrating in 1947 to the United States, where he joined the faculty at Yale as Sterling Professor of Romance Languages. The following extract is drawn from *Mimesis,* one of the most influential works of literary criticism of the twentieth century, and seeks to explain Stendhal's founding role in the development of modern realism by probing into his complex rejection of romantic Historicism.]

⟨. . .⟩ In his realistic writings, Stendhal everywhere deals with the reality which presents itself to him: *Je prends au hasard ce qui se trouve sur ma route,* ⟨. . .⟩ in his effort to understand men, he does not pick and choose among them; this method, as Montaigne knew, is the best for eliminating the arbitrariness of one's own constructions, and for surrendering oneself to reality as given. But the reality which he encountered was so constituted that, without permanent reference to the immense changes of the immediate past and without a premonitory searching after the imminent changes of the future, one could not represent it; all the human figures and all the human events in his work appear upon a ground politically and socially disturbed. ⟨. . .⟩ Insofar as the serious realism of modern times cannot represent man otherwise than as embedded in a total reality, political, social, and economic, which is concrete and constantly evolving—as is the case today in any novel or film—Stendhal is its founder.

However, the attitude from which Stendhal apprehends the world of event and attempts to reproduce it with all its interconnections is as yet hardly influenced by Historism—which, though it penetrated into France in his time, had little effect upon him. For that very reason we have referred in the last few pages to time-perspective and to a constant consciousness of changes and cataclysms, but not to a comprehension of evolutions. It is not too easy to describe Stendhal's inner attitude toward social phenomena. It is his aim to seize their every nuance; he most accurately represents the particular structure of any given milieu, he has no preconceived rationalistic system concerning the general factors which determine social life, nor any pattern-concept of how the ideal society ought to look; but in particulars his representation of events is oriented, wholly in the spirit of classic ethical psychology, upon an *analyse du cœur humain,* not upon discovery or premonitions of historical forces; we find rationalistic, empirical, sensual motifs in him, but hardly those of romantic Historism. Absolutism, religion and the Church, the privileges of rank, he regards very much as would an average protagonist of the Enlightenment, that is as a web of superstition, deceit, and intrigue; in general, artfully contrived intrigue (together with passion) plays a decisive role in his plot construction, while the historical forces which are the basis of it hardly appear. ⟨. . .⟩

On the other hand, he treats even the classes of society which, according to his views, should be closest to him, extremely critically and without a trace of the emotional values which romanticism attached to the word people. ⟨. . .⟩ No longer is birth or intelligence or the self-cultivation of the *honnête homme* the deciding factor—it is ability in some profession. This is no world in which Stendhal-Dominique can live and breathe. Of course, like his heroes, he too can work and work efficiently, when that is what is called for. But how can one take anything like practical professional work seriously in the long run! Love, music, passion, intrigue, heroism—these are the things that make life worthwhile.

> — Erich Auerbach, Mimesis: *The Representation of Reality in Western Literature,* trans. Willard R. Trask (Princeton: Princeton University Press, 1953): pp. 462–464.

℘

The Novel's Controversial Ending

[Giuseppi Tomasi di Lampedusa (1896–1957), a wealthy Sicilian prince as well as one of the great novelists of the twentieth-century, is known chiefly as the author of *The Leopard.* Here he vindicates *The Red and the Black,* arguing against the charge of excessive amorality readers have leveled at Stendhal for his portrayal of Julien, and against the complaint that the novel's ending is improbable.]

Ever since its publication, many people have been indignant over the author's indifference to morality. When, fifty years later, Stendhal's reputation began to skyrocket towards its present glory, people continued to be scandalized by the apology for unscrupulous ambition and by the lack of "soul" which they persisted in seeing in this "monster" Julien Sorel. Not long ago I heard it said that in *The Red and Black* one glimpses the tail of the devil.

Perhaps I am accustomed to the sight of that malignant tail which I see wriggling in every corner of my field of vision; the fact is that I have never been excessively shocked while reading the *Red and Black.* Julien Sorel has always appeared to me to be a shabby, over-ambitious young man, too devoid of scruples, it is true, too inclined to push forward in the shelter of his mistresses' skirts, but after all, nothing worse than what we can notice among a number of our acquaintances. And then, compared to a Dorian Gray, to Lafcadio, to Morel, and even to Reverend Slope, he is positively a little angel. I see some "bad" in him, but not an exceptional malignity. He is an everyday fellow; unusual only in that in the midst of a weak generation, he represents energy. I will say more: I see in him something pathetic, and in his creator a tendency to attribute responsibility for his misdeeds to historical circumstance.

It is undeniable, nevertheless, that the impression of vigorous amorality which emanates from the character is too diffuse to be excessive. In my opinion, it is a question of a misunderstanding born of this singularly perfect technique.

There are thousands of good-for-nothings like Julien in life and scores of them in art. Yet he is one of the rare ones who has been portrayed with a technique which places before the reader's eyes that malignity which really does not exceed the commonplace. A flea, magnified a hundred times, seems a monster of the apocalypse; one can admire the microscopist, but the flea remains a rather innocuous insect. It is not a matter of a monster, but of a character monstrously alive, much more alive than those of flesh and bone that we meet every day and whose hand we shake—without cordiality, but also without horror. Stendhal's technique has succeeded in laying Julien bare to the reader, that same Julien who to the other characters still seems to have a great number of qualities and several virtues. All nudities which are not those of Praxiteles are disgusting. But without them one does not learn anatomy.

Another complaint is made against the *Red and Black;* it is more serious because it concerns art. Numerous readers, and not ordinary readers, are disconcerted by Julien's end, which they find psychologically unjustified, technically careless, and aesthetically unsuccessful. I do not understand this opinion.

In the novel, the crisis, from the arrival of Mme de Rênal's letter onward, seems to me to be the inevitable consequence of Julien's character and actions. Could it have been different? The conclusion seems to me to be the most important part and I have already striven to explain why. We find in it not only the logical resolution of the situation, but also the honesty of genius in Stendhal, who no longer feels any interest in Julien from the moment when he has been *discovered*. The author hastens to kill the character in order to be free of him. It is a dramatic and evocative conclusion unlike any other.

— G. Tomasi di Lampedusa, "Notes sur Stendhal (*Le Rouge et le Noir*)," *Revue Stendhal-Club* 2. Reprinted in *Red and Black*, ed. Robert M. Adams (New York: W. W. Norton and Co., 1969): pp. 554–555.

THE PROBABILITY OF JULIEN'S CRIME

[Henri Martineau (1882–1958), described as the "dean of Stendhal scholars" by Robert M. Adams, is the author of *Le Coeur de Stendhal* and *L'Oeuvre de Stendhal,* from which the following comments are drawn. He argues against the view that "Julien's homicidal act" is not in keeping with his characteristic prudence and rationality. For Martineau, Julien's is a crime of passion that his impulsiveness, social awkwardness, class-conscious rage, and susceptibility to abrupt emotional change all help to contextualize and anticipate.]

Stendhal put too much skill, too much mastery, into the description of Julien's homicidal act, and into that return to passionate adoration of his victim which is the logical crown of his behavior, not to have been, at bottom, very well satisfied with himself.

And yet, I am not unaware this conclusion has appeared to some readers "rather strange, and in fact a little more contrived than is really legitimate."

These are the words of Emile Faguet, following upon his assertion that Stendhal is not intelligent. He pretends to show, further, that the pistol shot fired by Julien at Mme. de Rênal in the presence of an entire congregation was no more in the character of Julien Sorel than in the logic of events. ⟨. . .⟩

Certainly, the practical men who see in the hero of the *Red and Black* a prudent and calculating spirit will never forgive him for shattering, in a single instinctive gesture, the structure he has so painstak-ingly built up. The fact is, they treat Julien Sorel as a vulgar type of man-on-the-make, and want to see in him merely a success-chaser. That's their basic mistake. If you make that mistake, it's perfectly apparent you will never understand how a person who had meticu-lously managed his career, and was just about to pluck the fruits of his long and patient hypocrisy, could suddenly become foolish or pas-sionate enough to sacrifice everything to a momentary fury.

But can it be conceded that Julien Sorel is an artful dodger? Certainly not: throughout the book he is continually behaving awkwardly, against his own interests, and passion always prevails, in his soul, over calculation.

He devotes himself to hypocrisy simply because he has seen that it rules the world and imposes on credulous people by concealing all the worst weaknesses behind its smiling mask. But he himself is by no means, properly speaking, a hypocrite. He is a man of impulse, an extremely intelligent man of impulse who has come to understand the dangers of frankness in social life and who attempts to repress all his own impulses of loyalty, to throttle all the bold, wild impulses of youth which spring up so easily within him each time he forgets to stand guard over himself. ⟨. . .⟩

Neither a man of ambition nor a Tartufe, Julien is a young man whose social style is nearly always clumsy, to make use of Stendhal's own word. He is above all a plebeian in revolt, driven far less by the thought of immediate advantage to be gained than by a sense of outraged dignity and pride. And besides, he is absolutely deprived of any moral sense at all, and that is what shocked Faguet so much, and with good reason.

There's no cause for surprise, then, if this young man who is per-fectly spontaneous and just as capable of evil as of good decides in an access of rage to take revenge on Mme. de Rênal. He is all the more furious with her because at the bottom of his heart he has never ceased to cherish her. He brings against her all the resentments generated by a great love which has been betrayed. Is anything more needed to turn him to crime?

—Henri Martineau, *L'Oeuvre de Stendhal* (Paris: Albin Michel, 1951). Reprinted in *Red and Black,* ed. Robert M. Adams (New York: W. W. Norton and Co., 1969): pp. 446–448.

[Simone de Beauvoir (1908–1986)—existentialist philosopher, novelist, feminist, essayist—is best known for her
wide-ranging and challenging book *The Second Sex,* from
which the following extract is drawn. She discusses the
independence of Stendhal's female characters, an independence that their struggles against social, familial, and personal limitations help bring to light.]

⟨. . .⟩ This picture need only be reversed to show clearly what
Stendhal asks of women: it is first of all not to permit themselves to
be caught in the snares of seriousness; and because of the fact that
the things supposed to be of importance are out of their range,
women run less risk than men of getting lost in them; they have
better chances of preserving that naturalness, that naïveté, that generosity which Stendhal puts above all other merit. What he likes in
them is what today we call their authenticity: that is the common
trait in all the women he loved or lovingly invented; all are free and
true beings. ⟨. . .⟩

But it is in Mme de Rênal that independence of soul is most
deeply hidden; she is herself unaware that she is not fully resigned to
her lot; it is her extreme delicacy, her lively sensitivity, that show her
repugnance for the vulgarity of the people around her; she is
without hypocrisy; she has preserved a generous heart, capable of
violent emotions, and she has a flair for happiness. The heat of this
fire which is smoldering within her can hardly be felt from outside,
but a breath would be enough to set her all ablaze. ⟨. . .⟩

But liberty alone could hardly give them so many romantic attributes: pure liberty gives rise rather to esteem than to emotion; what
touches the feelings is the effort to reach liberty through the
obstructive forces that beat it down. It is the more moving in women
in that the struggle is more difficult. ⟨. . .⟩ Thus they have to invent a
thousand ruses to rejoin their lovers; secret doors, rope ladders,
bloodstained chests, abductions, seclusions, assassinations, outbursts
of passion and of disobedience are treated with the most intelligent
ingenuity; death and impending tortures add excitement to the
audacities of the mad souls he depicts for us. Even in his maturer
work Stendhal remains sensitive to this obvious romanticism: it is
the outward manifestation of what springs from the heart; they can

no more be distinguished from each other than a mouth can be separated from its smile. ⟨. . .⟩ The ladder that Mathilde de la Môle sets against her windowsill is no mere theatrical prop: it is, in tangible form, her proud imprudence, her taste for the extraordinary, her provocative courage. The qualities of these souls would not be displayed were they not surrounded by such inimical powers as prison walls, a ruler's will, a family's severity.

But the most difficult constraints to overcome are those which each person encounters within himself: here the adventure of liberty is most dubious, most poignant, most pungent. Clearly Stendhal's sympathy for his heroines is the greater the more closely they are confined. To be sure, he likes the strumpets, sublime or not, who have trampled upon the conventions once for all; but he cherishes Métilde more tenderly, held back as she is by her scruples and her modesty. ⟨. . .⟩ And Mme de Rênal, fettered by her pride, her prejudices, and her ignorance, is of all the women created by Stendhal perhaps the one who most astounds him. He frequently locates his heroines in a provincial, limited environment, under the control of a husband or an imbecile father; he is pleased to make them uncultured and even full of false notions. Mme de Rênal and Mme de Chasteller are both obstinately legitimist; the former is timid and without experience; the latter has a brilliant intelligence but does not appreciate its value; thus they are not responsible for their mistakes, but rather they are as much the victims of them as of institutions and the mores; and it is from error that the romantic blossoms forth, as poetry from frustration.

—Simone de Beauvoir, *The Second Sex,* ed. H. M. Parshley (New York: Alfred. A. Knopf, 1952; 1993): pp. 254–256.

⟨⟩

ELEMENTS OF REALISM

[Georges Blin taught Modern French literature at the Collège de France from 1965 to 1988. In addition to *Baudelaire,* and *Le Sadisme de Baudelaire,* he has written a pair of seminal studies of Stendhal—*Stendhal et les problèmes de la per-*

sonnalité and *Stendhal et les problèmes du roman,* from which this extract is taken. Blin discusses Stendhal's role in the development of the modern novel, contrasting his particular mode of realism to that of Balzac by examining the ways in which they incorporate descriptive detail into their writing.]

It can scarcely be denied that thanks to this close pictorial detail, these atmospheric qualities, in short this art of enveloping the narrative in the world of the senses, Stendhal provides sufficiently solid references in respect of external reality for him to be regarded as one of the founders, or at least as one of the clearest forerunners, of the modern novel. It only remains to be explained how anyone could ever have thought otherwise: how it is that this colouring, this precision, this suggestive orchestration of concrete detail escape the reader who does not consciously take stock. They do so, first, because this novelist tends to relegate to the background anything that smacks of strict 'realism': the painstaking application to detail that accuracy demands is something he prefers to save for the comic and the odious, whose functioning and portrayal remain of secondary importance, while he uses his own passionate involvement, and hence therefore ours, to breathe life into the lyrical and idealizing passion of his young protagonists: and, of course, it is they, as is only fitting, who receive the largest and most sharply focused share of the limelight. Thus, even when the novelist is led by his instinct for satire to describe things in detail, matters of the heart end up taking precedence over the demands of 'harsh reality'.⟨. . .⟩

Second, even when Stendhal consents to add one or two bold splashes of colour, the overall picture remains grey, and this is because he narrates in a hurry, shaping his sentences like arrows and leaving us little time to identify the tonalities he has employed: movement has no colour, while the pictorial is always static. But this is not all. If such a narrator never stops us in front of a picture, it is not just because of the accelerated way in which he makes us read, but for the very good reason that he is not painting a picture. A commentator assessing the amount of physical data used in *The Red and the Black* or in *Lucien Leuwen* can, by condensing them or listing them in sequence, create the false impression that a considerable measure of concrete reality has been involved in the way these novels treat their fictional stories. But during the telling of the story such touches were not so grouped, and the reader, for whom they were lost to view almost as soon as he encountered them, was never intuitively able to total them in such a way. This explains why, even when Stendhal provides enough physical traits (as accidental or necessary adjuncts of his story-telling) for us to be able to construct a portrait, the physical appearance of his characters is not what strikes us most. And the same goes for the landscapes. It is rare for him to leave us in complete ignorance of the settings, but he only reveals particular details (whether central or incidental) on separate occasions and in the diffuse order of a description whose progression is indistinguishable from that of the action itself. Thus, having never been able to take in the whole setting in one gaze, when we return to it we scarcely recognize it—something, moreover, which does no harm to the narrative since the author has managed to give us a reassuring if false sense of 'déjà vu'. Balzac, on the other hand, who anticipates the Naturalists in this respect, paints his portraits in great set-piece recapitulations, just as he groups together in comprehensive tableaux (where he alternates between simple lists and explanatory linkage) all the descriptive material he needs in order to establish, once and for all, his chosen milieu.

—Georges Blin, *Stendhal et les problèmes du roman* (Paris: José Corti, 1954). Reprinted in *Stendhal,* ed. Robert Pearson (London: Longman, 1994): pp. 72–73.

POLITICAL BACKGROUNDS OF THE NOVEL

[One of the most prominent American critics of the twentieth-century, Irving Howe (1920–1993) was a member of the "New York" school of intellectuals, which included Philip Rahv, Lionel Trilling, and Alfred Kazin. He is the author of *World of Our Fathers, Decline of the New, The Critical Point,* and *William Faulkner: A Critical Study.* Howe's comments in the following passage focus on the ways political movements in the background of *The Red and the Black* determine Julien's career and complicate his status as a hero.]

The Red and the Black is a novel about politics in an era which makes politics impossible. Though felt throughout the book as a directing energy, politics is seldom directly visible, except in the chapter where the nobles scheme to cauterize their country by entrusting it to English mercies. The society of *The Red and the Black* is not totalitarian, it enforces conformity through pressures rather than terrors. It is a society of pall even more than of fear, though its fear of the immediate past, of that free play of politics it has dedicated itself to suppress, is more than acute. In the absence of freedom, the political impulse takes the shape of ambition or hatred or banditry: all three stir in Julien Sorel. ⟨. . .⟩

Stendhal shows politics incarnated in non-political behavior, the struggle of the classes at a time when they lay dormant, crushed into a stupor of reconciliation. Nothing can appear directly in the world of this novel, nothing can be said openly: politics must break through in the guise of appetites, manners and sex. Julien Sorel is a man conducting a secret war against society, and a war that confuses him so much, for he has no firm base in principle, that he spends half his time conducting it against his mistresses and himself. ⟨. . .⟩ He is, as Stendhal says, "an unhappy man at war with all of society" but he cannot make proper distinctions among the various elements of society. He tells himself, "I will not follow the bourgeois, middle-of-the-road way of life, I seek rather some revolutionary exaltation," but this very exaltation, coming as it does in an age of social retreat, tempts him into crime. ⟨. . .⟩ Julien is the stranger in a hostile world but the stranger who no longer knows what he wants, who lacks, as Stendhal says, "the courage to be sincere." He is visited by libertarian emotions, he has moments of genuine compassion, but his major complaint against society is that it cramps him: he is bitter, above all, because it will not allow him to abandon, and perhaps betray, his own class.

The world as it presents itself to Julien Sorel is a battlefield: the battle has been fought and lost. Yet the image of warfare is crucial, for in no other 19th century novel is there such a formulated awareness that society has broken into warring classes. Every character in the book identifies himself with a special interest. "Between the liberty of the press and our existence as gentlemen," says M. de La Mole, spokesman for the nobles, "there is war to the knife." M. Renal, the rising bourgeois, cannot tolerate the thought that his rival has purchased two horses, and he finds relief only by hiring a tutor. That is the arithmetic of the bourgeois: two horses equals one tutor. And Julien himself, who thinks like a strange blend of Byron and Marx, begins his final speech to the jury almost—this seems to me a key to the novel—as if he were a *political* prisoner: "Gentlemen, I have not the honor to belong to your class . . ." If Julien could be transported to the Russia of a half century later, he would be a terrorist; given the necessity for living in Restoration France, which he can neither accept nor resist, he is hero, madman, clown. At the end he submits to his death in the consciousness, again like a political martyr, that he has already become a symbol.

—Irving Howe, *Politics and the Novel* (New York: Horizon Press, 1957): pp. 36–37.

⟨ঔ⟩

Julien's Parentage

[Robert M. Adams is the author of *Decadent Societies* and *Surface and Symbol,* and he has taught at Cornell University and the University of California at Los Angeles. In this excerpt from his classic study, *Stendhal: Notes on a Novelist,* Adams locates the vague matter of Julien's true parentage in the context of Stendhal's predilection for unresolved questions, open-ended subplots, and ambiguous details.]

⟨. . .⟩ Stendhal did not have many ideas; his abstract ideas were few and almost spectacularly limited. Henry Brulard is close to the truth when he remarks that "By instinct my moral life has been spent in careful consideration of five or six principal ideas, and in trying to see the truth about them" (Chapter 2). ⟨. . .⟩ One is reminded of Byron, who was great by virtue of his feelings. Stendhal too is better in the realm of feeling than in the realm of thought; but he is best of all in the realm of inexact observation. He had at his disposal immense resources of social situation; he was responsive to subtle nuances of impulse and behavior. And one of the qualities which contributes to his special gift is an ability to make thought reflect feeling and vice-versa—to frame a tale of deep and complex feelings which contrast with dry, clear, abstract ideas of the utmost obviousness—to show and to conceal himself with such adroitness that one is never sure how far one is to read beyond the printed page, only that there is somehow something more.

This indefinite recessing of the book beyond its ideas and beyond even the construct of its words constitutes a principal source of Stendhal's "impurity". He is in love with the open possibility, with the chance for whole new areas of life behind the areas described in the book; and he does nothing to close them off. Only consider as a single example the teasing which goes on throughout the *Rouge* regarding Julien Sorel's paternity. He is the son of old Sorel, a peasant carpenter; but he is something additional or something else. The Abbé Pirard thinks he is "the natural son of some rich man"; and when Julien takes naturally to Paris life asks "Can it be his blood coming out?" But then Norbert invents the same story for Julien, to account for his participation in a duel—that he is the illegitimate son of a wealthy nobleman in the Franche-Comté. M. de la Mole makes ironic and sceptical commentary on this story when he hears of it; when he gives Julien a cross, he gives him, for use with it, another pseudo-genealogy, he is to be the son of Duc de Retz; but later M. de la Mole tells the Abbé Pirard, apparently in all seriousness, "I know the truth about Julien's birth, and I authorize you not to keep this confidence secret."

⟨. . .⟩ In terms of the story, it does not much matter whether Julien is legitimate or illegitimate; what does matter is that Stendhal went to such pains to raise the issue in the reader's mind and to keep from closing it—that he left even his narrator in the dark (if he can be supposed to have had a distinct narrator; a sizable fragment of himself, if he cannot). A good ideologist, whose opinions on life in America, politics in novels, the novel as mirror, and other similar subjects are always ready to hand, might be expected to take a certain interest in obtaining clear and distinct ideas on a topic like his hero's paternity; but no, it is part of Stendhal's art to be full, clear, and explicit on topics which are immaterial, but to say nothing, or as little as possible, on matters where the busybody reader wants genuine, practical information.

—Robert M. Adams, *Stendhal: Notes on a Novelist* (New York: Funk and Wagnalls, 1959): pp. 71–74.

[Harry Levin (1912–1993) taught literature at Harvard University for many years and is the author of *The Question of Hamlet, Shakespeare and the Revolution of the Times,* and *The Gates of Horn,* from which this extract is taken. Levin analyzes how Stendhal's ironies allow him to negotiate between the categories of "realistic worldliness and romantic sensibility" that *The Red and the Black* puts in play.]

Though later generations of supermen and nihilists and *deracinés* and *immoralistes* pay their respects to Julien, and claim Stendhal as the founder of their *culte du moi,* no writer has more cogently insisted that egoism is self-destroying, and that the few cannot be happy when the many are unhappy. *Le Rouge et le noir,* accepted at its face value, could be made to serve as reactionary propaganda. Paul Bourget has sententiously retold the story in *Le Disciple:* his young upstart, influenced by the experimental doctrines of a philosopher modelled on Taine, seduces a young patrician and incites her to suicide. The labored moral is that new ideas are dangerous, and that the lower classes should be kept in their place. But face values are precisely what Stendhal wished to discount. "What the pride of the rich calls society" is for him a comic phenomenon; and while, in ironic footnotes, he disclaims the radical opinions of his characters, his own sympathies are with the interloper. The tragic resistance of the individual, vainly trying to uphold the integrity of his personality against the conformities and corruptions of the time, is what lends stature to Julien Sorel. At a time when it is difficult not to write satire, it is equally hard to be a hero; and Stendhal's irony fluctuates against the double standard of realistic worldliness and romantic sensibility. Julien surrenders too early and resists too late. The desperate intelligence that guides his steps, nevertheless, is a refutation of Amiel's criticism and an assertion of freedom of the will. ⟨. . .⟩

"Tender and honest" are Stendhal's adjectives for Julien, reconsidered at a distance of ten years, "ambitious, yet full of imagination and illusion." To be a lone champion of modernity, under a regimen which encouraged the shrewd and the stolid to adopt the costumes and revive the customs of the Middle Ages—surely Don Quixote was never confronted with a more preposterous situation. ⟨. . .⟩ In 1823 when the radical orator, Jacques Manuel, invoked the "new energy" that had emerged with the Revolution, he was expelled from the ultra-royalist Chamber of Deputies. This was the energy, submerged again during the Restoration, that Stendhal sought to register; the heat that soon, he warned his contemporaries, would be converted into force. Temporarily it lurked behind the comic mask, the clerical uniform, the antic disposition; Julien's hypocrisy, like Hamlet's madness, was a dramatic device. French logic had frequently speculated on the paradox of the comedian: Diderot maintained that the best acting had the least feeling, while Rousseau drew tragic implications out of Molière's ridicule. From the comedy of the nineteenth century to the tragedy is a step which Julien finally takes; his superiority, which must stoop to conquer, debases itself and foregoes its conquest. The irony of ironies is that Stendhal should pattern his hero upon the classic model of the hypocrite, that sincerity should be driven to *Tartufferie*. Yet Molière's comedy, which Julien committed to memory, had a special meaning for the Restoration; it voiced a protest against the clerical regime, which could not otherwise have been heard. Even Tartuffe had his great scene, when it befell the servant to order the master out of the house. To royalty and nobility, to the clergy and the Third Estate, to the thrones and powers and dominions and vested interests, *Le Rouge et le noir* brought back that scene with all the accelerating impact of a nightmare.

—Harry Levin, *The Gates of Horn* (New York: Oxford University Press, 1963): pp. 127–129.

JULIEN'S SELF-CONSCIOUSNESS

[A specialist in the French fiction of the last two centuries, Victor Brombert teaches literature at Princeton University. He is the author of *Stendhal et la voie oblique, The Intellectual Hero: Studies in the French Novel, 1880–1955,* and *The Novels of Flaubert,* among other works of criticism. In this extract from his important thematic study, *Stendhal: Fiction and the Themes of Freedom,* Brombert analyzes connections between seemingly contradictory aspects of Julien's character and the extent of his self-consciousness.]

Ambiguity extends, of course, to all aspects of Julien's character, specifically to those that involve tensions between individual and social values. At every point, the author introduces elements that destroy the mental picture the reader might be forming. This is particularly true of the early pages of the novel, where the hero's character begins to take shape. Julien's frenetic ambition seems to be summed up by his plebeian expression of horror at the thought of eating with the servants. ⟨. . .⟩ But no sooner has he made this proud and categorical statement than Stendhal informs us that this abhorrence of sharing meals with the servants was "not natural" to Julien, that it was bookish, that he in fact derived this repugnance from Rousseau's *Confessions*. Similarly, we learn in the same chapter of Julien's hypocritical visit to the church; but the very turn of phrase is tersely ambiguous. Julien considers that appearing in church for a quick prayer on his way to the Rênals' would be "useful for his hypocrisy". ⟨. . .⟩ But the need to perfect a role suggests that the role is not a congenital one. Only a fundamentally non-hypocritical person could thus decide, from the outside, to espouse the role of hypocrite, as though hypocrisy itself were a mask. ⟨. . .⟩

Conflict is at the heart of Stendhal's presentation, and it is of course at the heart of Julien's character. The tension is not merely between what Julien really is and what he would like to be; it involves dynamics that propel him to become what he is not and that lead to the discovery of what he becomes (and also remains) despite his self-imposed ambition. Timidity and resoluteness are constantly at war. The famous scene in the garden of Vergy, when Julien orders himself, in almost military style, to take Madame de Rênal's hand, describes the "awful battle raging between duty and timidity." There is comedy here too, for Julien is so taken with himself and with his tactical problems that he fails to notice his victory: Madame de Rênal, who has to get up for a moment, spontaneously returns her hand to him. This blindness is almost more significant than the battle between intrepidity and timorousness. It prefigures other states of hypnotic surrender to violent emotions and *idées fixes,* as in the Abbé Pirard's study or on his way back to Verrières to shoot Madame de Rênal. This blindness in the face of felicity—this inability to assess and possess the privileged moment—is one of the profound themes of the book. ⟨. . .⟩

But there is also honesty in this struggle with one's self, in this refusal to take anything for granted. The scepticism is in large part self-directed. ⟨. . .⟩ After the emotional tirade about Napoleon at the priest's dinner, he binds his right arm over his breast (a symbolic pose) and carries it in this painful position for two entire months. What emerges early in the book is a morality of multiple standards, in which the only standard that really counts is the privately established one, imposed with arbitrary self-discipline. Such ascetic demands made upon the self, without the comfort of objective, external guidance other than historical myths and literary images, are clearly related to a steady self-depreciation, which is another form of blindness. Julien both needs and fears the judgment of an external conscience. ⟨. . .⟩ Yet he does everything to camouflage his real feelings and to disguise his acts. He thus has only himself to rely on for criticism and reprimands. But he is persistently wrong about his feelings and, above all, charmingly unaware of his real qualities.

—Victor Brombert, *Stendhal: Fiction and the Themes of Freedom* (New York: Random House, 1968): pp. 70–73.

Julien's Fear of Self-Knowledge

[Michael Wood writes book and film reviews for *The New York Review of Books, The New York Times, The London Times,* and other periodicals, and teaches at Princeton University, where he is the Charles Barnwell Straut Professor of English. He is the author of *The Magician's Doubts: Nabokov and the Risks of Fiction, America in the Movies, Children of Silence,* and *Stendhal,* from which the following extract is drawn. Here Wood focuses on the crucial issue of Julien's relation to his own identity—how his impulse to self-invention tangles with his fear of self-knowledge.]

No one knows Julien, partly because Julien doesn't know himself, and partly because the character he presents is in any case an artifact, a composition, a montage of borrowed bits and pieces. The point about his using Rousseau as a model is not so much that the model should be Rousseau, although that does contribute a good deal to Julien's self-dramatizing style. The point is rather that he should be using a model at all, inventing himself by means of another person's reported life.

Stendhal has us guessing again, then. We can see that Julien really frightens people. Stendhal is careful to stress that this may be only a visual effect, Julien may just *look* scaring. And the resolution of this doubt is left hanging. We don't know the real Julien. Or rather we should not know the real Julien if he had not committed his crime. What we don't see in him, the zone of darkness in all his relations with other people, is the capacity, under special circumstances, to commit murder. His shooting of Mme de Rênal simultaneously answers all our questions about Julien and all his own questions about himself. Now we all know who he is.

The answer has to be violent and paradoxical because the repression is so profound. Julien wants to know who he is, but he is also afraid of knowing—above all of being known. He senses that the truth about himself may be ugly, and the two most disturbing moments in the book show us Julien confronted with a seriously intelligent gaze. First his father: 'Julien's great black and tear-filled eyes looked into the small mean grey eyes of the old carpenter, who seemed to want to peer down into the bottom of his soul'. There is a curious sense of brooding threat here. Later, the abbé Pirard, head of the seminary in Besançon, fixes a 'terrible eye' on Julien during his first interview. Julien faints. The ambiguity is complete. Shortly before this moment, Stendhal makes the remark I have already quoted about the effect of ugliness on a soul meant to appreciate beauty, so perhaps Julien passes out because he is so sensitive and Pirard is so scruffy and unappealing. Or perhaps he does it because he cannot bear this man to look at him in this way, because Pirard is a version of his father, the scrutinizing enemy eye. Sensibility, then, or a form of intuitive guilt, a refusal to acknowledge what Pirard might see in him. Stendhal, needless to say, is not going to tell us which.

We are close to the paradox which is at the heart of this shifting, delicate and yet curiously tight book. Julien Sorel, like most of us, wants to know who he is, but only on condition that he is who he wants to be. Otherwise he'd rather not know. As a result, the young Machiavelli of the Restoration, subtle and intriguing hero of the vestry and the bedroom, knows almost nothing either about himself or about his world. ⟨. . .⟩

—Michael Wood, *Stendhal* (Ithaca: Cornell University Press, 1971): pp. 77–78.

⟨℘⟩

JULIEN'S MOTIVES FOR MURDER

[D. A. Miller has taught at the University of California at Berkeley and currently is on the faculty at Columbia University. An authority on nineteenth-century fiction, his works include *The Novel and the Police, Bringing Out Roland Barthes,* and *Narrative and Its Discontents,* from which the comments that follow are drawn. Miller complicates the commonplace view of Julien's ambitiousness by interpreting his attempt on Mme. de Rênal's life as an "attempt to save what she meant to him," an attempt to redress the injustice her letter seems to do to the memory of their relationship.]

Julien's most conspicuous lapse, surely, is his decision to "avenge" himself on Mme de Rênal—because she has maligned him in a letter to the marquis de la Mole, who as a result has repudiated him. ⟨. . .⟩ From the standpoint of Julien's ambition, no move could be more unwise than his attempt to shoot his former mistress. Yet the initial shock of the marquis' fury reaches him, paradoxically, "in the midst of transports of the most unbridled ambition." At the very moment when he would seem most committed to the spoils of ambition, he perversely acts to despoil himself.

One might recall, however, that Julien has himself solicited Mme de Rênal's letter. The marquis writes in uncomprehending rage, "L'impudent m'avait engagé lui-même à écrire à Mme de Rênal." It is as though Julien unconsciously sought in the letter another "souvenir": a disguised remembrance of a love whose value has seemed to increase with the distance of retrospection from which it is viewed. Yet even souvenirs, it would now appear, have changed color. ⟨. . .⟩

In an obvious sense, the letter is grossly unfair, even to the point of exaggerating Julien's tactical abilities. "The most consummate hypocrisy" seems an extravagant formula with which to designate the naive, clumsily enforced bluffing that went into the seduction of Mme de Rênal and Mathilde. Yet if the letter is not true in the sense of conforming to the full portrait of Julien drawn by the novel, it just fits the facts and it offers a different way in which these facts might be seen. Muddle is erected into system, and incidental effects treated as manifest intentions. The letter's reductiveness drains Julien's career of his own particular relationship to it, and so confers on it all the coherence that his depth of feeling had tended to disperse. By significant omission, the letter brings into question the very existence of such feeling. This is a souvenir that refuses to function as such. It says, in effect, that the event to which it testifies never really happened—Julien has never been there.

His attempt to destroy Mme de Rênal, then, is an extreme attempt to save what she has meant to him—to put her back in her place at the dead center of red. At the same time, it forcefully rejects the spirit of the letter, adding a new fact to the biography that the readings of hypocrisy and ambition cannot well account for. Most important, this unlawful act (in a double sense: both against the law and against the rules of his own game) brings about the final reunion of Julien and Mme de Rênal, a reunion invested with the only values that now matter. Under their pressure, Julien dismisses his past plotting as an irrelevant diversion, and with it much of the novel. ⟨. . .⟩

—D. A. Miller, *Narrative and Its Discontents* (Princeton: Princeton University Press, 1981): pp. 203–205.

⊗

PATERNITY AND AUTHORITY

[Peter Brooks teaches literature at Yale University. His publications include *The Melodramatic Imagination, The Novel of Worldliness,* and *Reading for the Plot,* the classic study from which the following extract is taken. Here Brooks examines the relation between paternity and authority in *The Red and the Black,* suggesting that Julien's story resists authority in all the forms in which the novel represents it, from M. de Rênal to M. de La Mole to the narrator himself.]

To Julien's generation of his narrative from fictional models we can juxtapose the seriality of those figures of paternity who claim authority in his career. He is set in relationship to a series of ideal or possible fathers, but in a curious manner whereby each father figure claims authority, or has authority conferred on him, at just the moment when he is about to be replaced. The "real," or at least legal, father, Sorel the carpenter, is already well on the way to repudiation when the novel opens; his first replacement, the chirurgien-major who has bequeathed his Legion of Honor to Julien, is dead and his legacy suppressed in the movement from red to black. The paternity of the Abbé Chélan emerges in strong outline only when Julien has left him for the seminary, where the severe Abbé Pirard will eventually address Julien as *filius.* "I was hated by my father from the cradle," Julien will say to Pirard, "this was one of my greatest misfortunes; but I will no longer complain of fortune, I have found another father in you, sir." Yet this moment of overt recognition comes only in Chapter 1 of Book 2, that is, after Julien's translation to Paris and his establishment in the Hôtel de la Mole: precisely the moment when Pirard begins to give way to the Marquis de la Mole, who will complicate the question of paternity and play out its various transformations. ⟨. . .⟩

But I have so far said nothing about another figure of paternal authority in the narrative: the narrator. The relation of the narrator to Julien—and of all Stendhalian narrators to the young protagonists of his novels—is patently paternalistic, a mixture of censure and indulgence; the narrator sets a standard of worldly wisdom that the protagonist must repeatedly violate, yet confesses to a secret admiration for the violation, especially for *l'imprévu,* the unforeseeable, the moments when Julien breaks with the very notion of model and pattern. The narrator constantly judges Julien in relation to his chosen models, measuring his distance from them, noting his failures to understand them, his false attributions of success to them, and the fictionality of the constructions he builds from them. ⟨. . .⟩ This obtrusive narrator, master of every consciousness in the novel, claims to demonstrate why things necessarily happened the way they did, yet inevitably he suggests the arbitrariness and contingency of every narrative turn of events, how easily it might have been otherwise. ⟨. . .⟩

The issue of authority, in all its manifestations, remains unresolved. Julien achieves no final relationship to any of his figures of paternity. It is indeed Sorel the carpenter who re-emerges in the place of the father at the end, and Julien attributes to him the jolly thought that the expectation of a legacy of three or four hundred louis from his son will make him, like any father, happy to have that son guillotined. The fathers inherit from the sons. As for Julien's own paternity, his plan that Mme de Rênal take care of his son—whom Mathilde will neglect—goes for naught when Mme de Rênal dies three days after he does. The fate of this son—if son it be—never is known. The novel rejects not only specific fathers and authorities but the very model of authority, refusing to subscribe to paternity as an authorizing figure of novelistic relationships. ⟨. . .⟩

—Peter Brooks, *Reading for the Plot* (New York: Alfred A. Knopf, 1984): pp. 73, 75, 87.

EPISTOLARY TRADITION

[Margaret Mauldon has recently published acclaimed translations of *The Charterhouse of Parma* and Huysmans's *Against Nature*. In this excerpt she situates Julien's courtship of Mme. de Fervaques in the context of Stendhal's response to the tradition of the epistolary novel, a response informed by an awareness of epistolary correspondence as a tool for manipulation and deception.]

After Mathilde breaks off their relationship Julien resorts to devious epistolary tactics in order to regain her love. He painstakingly copies out and delivers to Mme de Fervaques's home the fifty-three model letters provided by his mentor prince Korasoff, following the prescribed programme of courtship with tenacious exactitude. The satire of the epistolary code is here overt, since the precise instructions regarding the manner of delivering the letters, their timing and length, and the careful gradation of their contents are all guaranteed to be efficacious regardless of circumstances. In fact, so totally unrelated to reality are these letters that when Julien forgets to alter the details of place names in the originals—which were addressed to an English quakeress—no harm is done. Julien does not bother to open, let alone read, the replies he receives from Mme de Fervaques. Mathilde's resistance breaks down when she discovers a pile of these unopened letters in Julien's bureau drawer. This episode reduces to the level of absurdity the notion of epistolary courtship. The letters sent by Julien are devoid of real content; they have meaning only as tokens of exchange in an accepted social ritual. But here again Julien uses an epistolary manœuvre for his own purposes. The writing of these interminable letters does indeed convey a message, but it is a message directed at Mathilde. The traditional concept of seduction by letter is turned inside out in this narrative sequence, its only meaning that of an empty ritualized gesture, its true purpose the seduction of a lady who is never addressed.

In conclusion I should like to widen the focus of my remarks and consider the function of epistolary incidents within the economy of the entire narrative. One way of reading *Le Rouge et le Noir* is to see it as a contrapuntal exploration of the differing levels of insincerity which characterize communication both *between* individuals and also *within* the mind of a single individual. As Julien learns to recognize and to exploit the varied ways in which the world presents itself to his consciousness, not only does he learn how to use society, he learns also, though without realizing it, that society can never give him what he desires. When, during his last days in prison, Julien is isolated from the world, he discovers that nothing matters expect the love he and Mme de Rênal share.

I would suggest that there is a connection between the final lesson Julien learns and the fact that, in recording his hero's accession to this truth, Stendhal parodies the epistolary form. The epistolary mode is essentially a social mode of expression. It seemingly offers, at least to the naïve reader, the illusion that language is transparent and can be used for unmediated communication. But it is not surprising that *Les Liaisons dangereuses* should be the last of the great epistolary works. Laclos's novel demonstrates with relentless logic the way language can always function as a tool of persuasion and deception, both of the 'other' and of the self. It exploits to the limit the potential of epistolary narrative, and contains the seeds of its decay. Stendhal learned the lesson Laclos had taught. It is no accident that in *Le Rouge et le Noir* he should so entertainingly expose the conceptual flaws and technical ineptitudes of a narrative mode which had originally proposed a deceptively optimistic view of the nature of language. *Le Rouge et le Noir* is in fact a catalogue of miscommunications: of misleading roles assumed or imposed, of mistaken identities, of misunderstandings, misrepresentations and misreadings.

> —Margaret Mauldon, "Generic Survival: *Le Rouge et le Noir* and the Epistolary Tradition," *French Studies* 38, no. 4 (October 1984): pp. 420–421.

☙

THE PRACTICE OF RECITATION

> [Christopher Prendergast is Professor of Modern French Literature at King's College, Cambridge, and is the author of *Balzac: Fiction and Melodrama,* and *Paris and the Nineteenth Century.* Here he examines the social codes—provincial, ecclesiastic, aristocratic—that inform the novel. Prendergast suggests that Julien's comeuppance is achieved by way of a strategy of "recitation" that paradoxically allows him a measure of freedom from conversational, behavioral, and epistolary orthodoxies even as it represents his submission to them.]

⟨...⟩ The return of the Bourbons, the restoration of the authority of the Church, the influence of the Académie and the salons, the proliferation of censors and spies, all conspire to re-imprison discourse within the orthodox grip of Opinion. Stendhal's career as a novelist, and that of his heroes within the novels, are indelibly marked by that loss. Their aversion from the idioms of the time is notorious: Stendhal's pronounced reluctance in *Le Rouge et le Noir* to recount the terms of provincial conversation; Julien's disdain for the banalities of every milieu in which he finds himself. Yet for the author of *Le Rouge et le Noir,* the reproduction of these idioms is indispensable to the notion of the novel as a 'chronique due XIXe siècle', and their mastery a necessary condition of the hero's progress. The stake, and the ruse, of both author and hero in *Le Rouge et le Noir* is how to retain some vestige of freedom while negotiating what threatens that freedom: how Julien speaks to the other characters and how Stendhal speaks to his readers are two faces of the same dilemma and the same game.

One way of describing *Le Rouge et le Noir* is as an ensemble of discourses or, in Barthes's term, 'sociolects', each of which corresponds to a particular social group, and which together furnish the different 'scripts' with which Julien acts out his various roles. ⟨. . .⟩ there are essentially three such forms: the discourse of Verrières and the provincial bourgeoisie, of the Church and the Besançon seminary, and of the aristocratic salon in Paris. Julien's 'journey' is a movement through this sociolectal universe in a determined, if somewhat discontinuous, process of adaptation and accommodation. For, contrary to his Napoleonic fantasy of a self realized in action, Julien makes his way in the world less through deeds than through words, and it is precisely his education in these terms that gives one of the novel's ironic comments on the fact that in the society of the Restoration significant forms of action are no longer available. ⟨. . .⟩ Most of the advice Julien receives (from Abbé Pirard, Prince Korasoff) centres not so much on what he should do as on what he should say (and not say), while many of his own self-admonitions are reflections on the importance of specifically verbal strategies. ⟨. . .⟩ His conquest of society consists largely in learning to manipulate social codes of speech, in acquiring arts of verbal dissimulation through which an accommodating and acceptable public self can be presented to the world. ⟨. . .⟩ Through a series of studied verbal 'performances', modelled on the socially recognized idioms, he constantly seeks, though sometimes fails, to adjust his visible self to the expectations of others, and, in this way, to forge a secure place for himself in the world.

'Performance' can be taken here in a quite literal sense. Julien's basic relation to the standard discourses of his society is one of *recitation*, parodied in that grotesque recital from memory of long stretches of the Bible which so impresses the Valenod family. ⟨. . .⟩

—Christopher Prendergast, *The Order of Mimesis: Balzac, Stendhal, Nerval, Flaubert* (Cambridge: Cambridge University Press, 1986). Reprinted in *Stendhal,* ed. Robert Pearson (London: Longman, 1994): pp. 231–232.

Plot Summary of
The Charterhouse of Parma

Stendhal composed *The Charterhouse of Parma,* his last completed novel, by dictation in just over seven weeks in 1838. He based the narrative on an account of the life of Alessandro Farnese that he discovered in a manuscript compendium of Renaissance Italian tales, which he was translating and reworking for publication. Stendhal adapted the tale as a "romanzetto," but later developed it as a full-length novel, inspired perhaps by the challenge of transposing it into the nineteenth-century. Its rapid production and origins in a quasi-history of sensationalized intrigues hover over its early reception: in an otherwise celebratory review, Balzac lamented Stendhal's "glaring" inattention to diction and grammar, while Henry James, who also praised the novel, worried over its "grossly immoral" characters, recommending it only to readers of solid moral conviction. The novel's unique blend of quixotic adventure and psychological analysis, tragedy and humor, romance and political satire, has continued to complicate its interpretation even as it has ensured its gradual emergence as an undisputed masterpiece.

The Charterhouse of Parma opens at the turn of the nineteenth century in northern Italian territories caught between the warring French and Austrian empires. Napoleon's arrival in Milan ushers in a period of "pleasure and happiness" that drives the Marchese del Dongo, an aristocratic reactionary, into hiding on his country estate at Grianta, an absence that paves the way for his wife's adulterous union with Lieutenant Robert, a French army officer, who fathers Fabrizio del Dongo, the novel's protagonist. Recalled by his father from the pleasures of Milan and the company of his aunt, the Countess Pietranera, Fabrizio is entrusted to the Abbé Blanès, who is more an astrologer than a Latinist, to finish an education already weakened by his reliance on his aunt's influence with his superiors at school. Following Napoleon's fall in 1813, the death of the Countess's husband occasions her retreat to Grianta, where she bonds with Fabrizio and vacations with the Marchesa in Milan. Inspired by the sight of an eagle he takes for an omen, Fabrizio decides to join the French army when he learns of Napoleon's recent landing in Italy.

Misfortune dogs Fabrizio throughout his attempt to serve Napoleon, in spite of the money his mother supplies him with and the variety of identities he conveniently assumes. Taken for a spy, he is imprisoned arriving in Paris and released only through the generosity of the jailer's wife. He is befriended at Waterloo by a canteen-woman who helps him to join Marshall Ney's regiment. His confused experience under Ney and later under Corporal Aubrey leave him wondering whether or not he really saw action and disillusioned with his ideals of military glory. After surviving an altercation with French cavalrymen during a stint as a sentry, he convalesces at the house of a Flemish farmer, whose daughter and Fabrizio share a brief romance. He makes his way home and, after a chance meeting with Clélia Conti that foreshadows his later passion for her, he journeys to Romagnano, having been denounced by his brother Ascanio to the Milanese police.

Despite her growing feelings for her nephew, the Countess accepts the advances of Count Mosca, a Minister under Prince Ranuccio-Ernesto IV. Through a marriage of convenience to an elderly Duke, she becomes the Duchess Sanseverina and, with the exception of a faction led by Marchesa Raversi, proceeds to endear herself to the aristocracy of Parma. Assuming roles as Fabrizio's guardians, the Duchess and the Count persuade him to enroll in the Ecclesiastical Academy at Naples, from which he returns four years later a Monsignore possessed of an adult reserve and nobility that appeal to his aunt and prompt Mosca's jealousy. In spite of his success at court, Fabrizio feels troubled by his consciousness of the Duchess's feelings for him and travels back to Grianta, where he visits Abbé Blanès. Still at odds with Ascanio, who keeps the police on the lookout for him, Fabrizio makes a precarious escape back to Parma, where he learns that the Duchess's husband has died, leaving her a huge inheritance. As Fabrizio recounts his escape to Mosca and the Duchess, he begins to feel haunted by the Abbé's ominous pronouncement that he must resist a "violent temptation that will seem justified by the laws of honor" in order to achieve happiness.

Fabrizio offers to oversee Mosca's excavation project at Sanguigna as a token of his appreciation for the Count's efforts in securing him the favor of Archbishop Landriani, who hopes to make Fabrizio his Coadjutor. While at Sanguigna he crosses paths with his mistress Marietta and her protector Giletti, members of an acting troupe recently banished from Parma. Fabrizio vanquishes Giletti and then flees for the Austrian border. Ludovico, a former servant of the Duchess's, helps Fabrizio to escape to Ferrara and thence to Bologna. There he receives word of Marchesa Raversi's intention to calumniate him by twisting the story of Giletti's death by alleging that Fabrizio paid the excavation workers to assist him with the murder.

Pricked on by his sense of vanity, Fabrizio decides to pursue the heart of Fausta, a popular singer and the beloved of an arrogant young Count. He follows the couple to Parma, continues to court Fausta, and is placed under arrest by the Count, who believes him to be the Prince and intends to embarrass him. Fabrizio escapes, and after taking revenge on the Count in a duel, flees to Bologna. Meanwhile, the Raversi faction's steady progress in developing their case against Fabrizio encourages the Duchess to leave Parma, but the Prince, concerned about the liveliness of court life in her absence, persuades her to stay by agreeing to pardon her nephew. Fabrizio enters the Farnese Tower, which is under the administration of Fabio Conti, whose palace is adjacent to it. Upset by Fabrizio's imprisonment and disappointed by the cowardly display of courtly propriety that brought Mosca to leave out a crucial clause in her agreement with the Prince, the Duchess breaks with the Count.

Intent on making up for his mistake, Mosca promises to ennoble Chief Justice Rassi in exchange for information about the Prince's plans for Fabrizio, but is not able to do much for him. Much as it does for Julien Sorel in *The Red and the Black,* the prison proves a place of regeneration for Fabrizio, whose window faces that of Clélia's aviary and thus allows them to communicate using improvised signals and letters. Her sense of propriety does not permit her to avow her feelings for him, though Fabrizio falls eagerly and openly in love with her. Under pressure from her father either to wed the wealthy Marchese Crescenzi or enter a convent, Clélia delays her decision so as to remain close to Fabrizio. Torn by a telling jealousy of the Duchess, a deep remorse at neglecting her duty to her father, and a growing affection for Fabrizio, she makes preventing his enemies' attempts to poison him her first priority. Meanwhile, Fabrizio learns from the Duchess that the certainty of an attempt on his life makes his immediate escape compulsory, but fearing he would never see Clélia once out of prison, he resolves to stay.

The Duchess devises a safe means of escape with the help of Ferrante Palla, a doctor, poet, revolutionary, and highway robber who, wholly enamored of her, pledges himself to her service. After they test a plan of escape on a local ruin, Palla, Sanseverina, and Clélia secretly deliver ropes to Fabrizio, though part of the delivery involves drugging Fabio Conti – an episode that aggravates his daughter's guilt at betraying him. Fabrizio escapes successfully thanks to a fortuitous fog and the drunkenness of the guards. He flees with the Duchess across the Po to Piedmont, but his distance from Clélia depresses him visibly, causing his aunt to reflect on her fading beauty and to wonder jealously whom he might love. Back in Parma, the Duchess has the Prince quietly murdered. Together with Mosca, whom she marries, she arranges a just trial for Fabrizio, who then comes back to Parma, returning to the Farnese Tower because of his desire to see Clélia. Aware of the danger of Fabio Conti's vengeance, the Duchess negotiates desperately with Ernesto V, agreeing to a rendezvous with him in exchange for Fabrizio's freedom. He is later acquitted and made Coadjutor, though his success in high society does little to alleviate his despair on finding Clélia living reclusively with her aunt, and so soon after she showed such a clear devotion to him on the day of his rescue.

Although Fabrizio manages to visit Clélia and they confirm their mutual love, Clélia marries Crescenzi out of duty to her father. Fabrizio begins a religious retreat, avoiding society occasions and gaining a reputation for sanctity. Forced to make an appearance one evening at the Prince's palace, he encounters Clélia, whose fears that he no longer loves her are assuaged when he quotes her some Petrarchan verses. She offers him her fan as a token of friendship, and Fabrizio immediately resolves to rejoin court life. The Duchess marries Mosca, joining him in Perugia following her promised rendezvous with the Prince, and Fabrizio circulates in society in order to keep the couple posted on town news out of gratitude for their efforts on his behalf. He begins to preach, becoming famous for it due to the inspiration he derives from imagining the possibility of drawing Clélia to his church. Annetta Marini, a young beauty in his congregation, falls in love with Fabrizio, inciting Clélia's jealousy. Eventually Clélia rationalizes a visit to Fabrizio's church, and the day after his sermon invites him to meet her in the orangery of the Palazzo Crescenzi, where, under the cover of darkness, she can keep her vow never to see him without forfeiting his company altogether. Years later, with Mosca reinstated in the Parma government, Fabrizio demands custody of his son Sandrino from Clélia, the boy's mother, but Sandrino dies several months later, and Clélia dies in Fabrizio's arms not long after. Having divided his fortune between his mother and the Duchess, Fabrizio, saddened by the loss of his lover, retires to the Charterhouse of Parma. ❀

List of Characters in
The Charterhouse of Parma

Probably the natural son of Lieutenant Robert, **Fabrizio del Dongo** is the heir of the Marchese del Dongo, a greedy aristocrat whom he defies by attempting to join Napoleon at Waterloo—a rebellious act that attests to his quixotic character and sparks Gina's passion for him. Handsome, intelligent, and impulsive, he is also possessed of an unselfconscious nobility that sometimes shades into selfish arrogance: he believes himself "created to be happier than other men" and accepts as a matter of course his advancement in the hierarchy of the church. While in prison for murdering the actor Giletti, he falls in love with Clélia Conti, thus putting to rest his doubts about his susceptibility to genuine romantic passion. The novel turns tragic as Fabrizio's sense of disillusionment develops, and his final withdrawal to the Charterhouse of Parma represents a return to the idea of fulfillment in self-confinement evoked by his experience in the Farnese Tower.

Gina Pietranera, the Duchess Sanseverina, was in Balzac's judgment the novel's most memorable character, "a Diana endowed with the sensual appeal of a Venus, the sweetness of Raphael's virgins, and the animated vigor of Italian passion." Her beauty, wit, and spontaneity make her immensely popular at court, but her success is overshadowed by her unrequited love for Fabrizio. She becomes the Duchess Sanseverina through a purely formal marriage arranged by Count Mosca, with whom she works indefatigably to secure Fabrizio's fortunes and whose advances she accepts without ever relinquishing her primary attachment to her nephew. Largely oblivious to social decorum, she has a theatrical flair that shows in her negotiations with Ernesto IV, whom she orders Ferrante Palla to murder, and his successor Ernesto V, to whom she sacrifices her virtue in exchange for Fabrizio's freedom. Widowed a second time, she marries Mosca and temporarily retires from court life, eventually coming to reside on the Austrian side of the Po, where she passes her last days hosting the high society of Parma.

Count Mosca, a middle-aged courtier with cheerful manners and a knack for sparing the Prince from embarrassment, enters the narrative as an impassioned and eventually successful suitor to Gina

Pietranera. A veteran of Napoleonic campaigns, he treats court life like a sordid game, and his readiness to resign his government position charms Gina, whom he marries despite the temporary rift caused by a momentary yielding to courtly propriety that jeopardizes her plans to help Fabrizio. His relationship with Gina focuses the novel's exploration of themes of youth and old age. The fatherly regard he shows Fabrizio is complicated by feelings of jealousy that on one occasion nearly prompt him to have the young Monsignore done away with, an impulse that accords with his subtle self-centeredness: "He considered himself obliged to seek above all the happiness of Count Mosca della Rovere."

Clélia Conti, the daughter of the jailer Fabio Conti, falls in love with Fabrizio during his time in prison. Her "celestial beauty" reflects her "lofty soul," and she scorns the vulgarity of worldly existence, practicing her religion with tremendous earnestness. Her piety and sense of duty to her father, whom she betrays by helping Fabrizio to escape, cause her to feel great remorse, and she vows never to lay eyes on her lover. Typical of representations of love in Stendhal's oeuvre, the romance between Clélia and Fabrizio is connected to a process of overcoming obstacles, as their communication by signals, songs, alphabets, and letters during his imprisonment points up. She marries the Marchese Crescenzi, but her passion for Fabrizio is reawakened when she attends one of his sermons, and she arranges to meet him by night so as not to break her vow. Their romance borrows the accents of Shakespeare's *Romeo and Juliet,* and the conclusion of their relationship is fittingly tragic, as Clélia passes away in her lover's arms following the death of Sandrino, their son.

Ranuccio-Ernesto IV, the Prince of Parma, sits at the center of a royalist court that presents a satirical tableau of post-Napoleonic political life. Haunted by his role in having a pair of liberals executed, he relies heavily on Mosca's prudence and diplomacy to keep his paranoia under control. Like many of Stendhal's high-ranking officials, Ernesto IV is burdened by ennui and anxieties regarding further advancement. Though he possesses a degree of majesty, he keeps a harsh prison and presides over a corrupt administration. He meets his end at the hands of Ferrante Palla, commissioned by the Duchess to murder the Prince for his treatment of Fabrizio.

A doctor, poet, and revolutionary, **Ferrante Palla** practices a restricted form of highway robbery in order to make ends meet.

Rumored to be insane, he falls in love with the Duchess and pledges himself to her service. It is Palla who evolves the plan for Fabrizio's escape "by means of ropes"—a plan he himself tests on a medieval ruin resembling the Farnese Tower before recommending it to the Duchess. He assassinates the Prince on the Duchess's command and, devoted to republican ideals, leads a short-lived revolt in Parma that is soon suppressed by Count Mosca.

Chief Justice Rassi is "a perfect courtier: without honor and without humor." Servile in the extreme, his chief passion is "to converse intimately with great personages and to entertain them by his buffooneries." He is an expert in legal matters in addition to being resourceful and intelligent, and he makes himself indispensable to the Prince, who keeps him in his employ but shows him no respect, frequently insulting and even beating him. A member of the court faction that opposes the interests of Mosca and the Duchess, he accepts the titles the Count offers him in exchange for information regarding the Prince's plans for Fabrizio.

Ranuccio-Ernesto V succeeds Ranuccio-Ernesto IV, his father, who is murdered by Ferrante Palla at the Duchess's behest. Priding himself on "a moral ministry," he naively believes his government to be immune to corruption and is baffled by the Duchess's fears for Fabrizio's safety in prison. Enamored of the Duchess, he extracts from her a promise for a rendezvous in exchange for Fabrizio's freedom, a promise he later demands that she honor in spite of the desperate circumstances under which it was made. Innocent and kind-hearted but cowardly, he eventually comes to be "adored by his subjects," who compare "his government to that of the Grand Dukes of Tuscany." ❈

Critical Views on
The Charterhouse of Parma

NOVEL'S VIRTUES AND FLAWS

[Honoré de Balzac (1799–1850), probably the greatest novelist of his time, is the author of such classics as *Lost Illusions, Old Goriot,* and *Cousin Bette,* and is considered, with Stendhal, to be the founder of modern realism. He lavishes considerable praise on *The Charterhouse of Parma* in his influential review, from which the following passages are drawn. He compares the novel to *The Prince*, critiques Stendhal's stylistic inadequacies, and compliments his skills both in drawing characters and handling ideas.]

M. Beyle has written a book in which the sublime blazes forth from chapter after chapter. He has produced—at an age when men rarely even think of large-scale subjects to write about, and having already written some twenty extremely amusing and intelligent volumes—a work which can be appreciated only by people, souls, of a truly superior kind. In short, he has written *The Modern Prince,* the novel that Machiavelli would write if he were alive today and living in exile from Italy. ⟨. . .⟩

The Duchess is like one of those magnificent statues which fill one with admiration for their art while at the same time making one curse nature for being so sparing with the real-life models on which they are based. When you have read the book, Gina will remain before your eyes like a sublime statue: neither the Venus de Milo, nor the Medici Venus, but a Diana endowed with the sensual appeal of a Venus, the sweetness of Raphael's virgins, and the animated vigour of Italian passion. Above all there is nothing French about the Duchess. No, the Frenchman who has made this model and carved and polished the marble has brought nothing of his homeland to this work. ⟨. . .⟩ You will see greatness in her, you will find her witty and intelligent, passionate, always authentic, and yet the author has carefully concealed the sensual side of her being. There is not a single word in the book to suggest the sensuality of love or to arouse it. Although the Duchess, Mosca, Fabrice, the Prince and his son, Clélia, although the whole book and its characters represent, in one way or another, all the storms of passion, and although this is Italy as she really is, with all the finesse, the play-acting, the cunning, the sang-froid, the tenacity, where the art of high politics is applied in every circumstance, *The Charterhouse of Parma* is a novel more chaste than the most puritan of Walter Scott's. To create someone noble, larger than life, well-nigh irreproachable, out of a duchess who brings happiness to a Mosca and keeps nothing from him, out of an aunt who adores her nephew Fabrice, is that not the work of a master? ⟨. . .⟩

The weakness of the work lies in the style, that is, in the way the words are combined (for the thought behind them, being eminently French, holds the sentences together). The mistakes which M. Beyle makes are purely grammatical: he is negligent and inaccurate in the manner of seventeenth-century writers. ⟨. . .⟩ But if the French language is like a coat of varnish applied to thought, then one must be as indulgent towards those in whom the varnish is spread over beautiful paintings as one is severe towards those in whom one sees only the varnish. If in the case of M. Beyle the varnish has yellowed somewhat in places and cracked in others, it nevertheless allows one to make out a sequence of thoughts which follow on from each other according to the laws of logic. ⟨. . .⟩ But the ideas behind it all are substantial and vigorous, and the thinking is original and often well carried through. This is not a system to be imitated: it would be much too dangerous a thing to let authors see themselves as profound thinkers.

What saves M. Beyle is the depth of feeling which animates his thinking. All those to whom Italy is dear, who have studied or understood her, will read *The Charterhouse* with delight. ⟨. . .⟩

—Honoré de Balzac, *Revue parisienne* 25 Sept. 1840. Reprinted in *Stendhal*, ed. Robert Pearson (London: Longman, 1994): pp. 33–35.

[Emile Faguet (1847–1916) served as drama critic of the *Journal des Débats* and authored several acclaimed chronological surveys of French literature. Here he interprets *The Charterhouse of Parma* as a re-writing of *The Red and the Black,* and suggests that in spite of the power of the ending of the *Charterhouse,* he prefers the earlier novel because its hero, Julien Sorel, is more complexly motivated than Fabrizio.]

The Charterhouse of Parma is a kind of copy of *The Red and the Black:* same general idea, same characters, different surroundings and scenery. But the main idea is presented with less force, and the protagonists have, as it were, had their corners softened and their edges smoothed: thoughts and characters all stand out less. It is as if a second impression had been made from a worn woodcut. An ambitious young Frenchman of 1815: *The Red and the Black;* an ambitious young Italian of 1815: *The Charterhouse of Parma.* [. . .] As with Julien, Fabrice's initial enthusiasm for war is followed by the resolve to embark on an ecclesiastical career and to follow the twisting paths of intrigue, as he becomes both hypocrite and diplomat and takes the **cardinal de Retz** as his model. But, being born into the aristocracy and protected by the mistress of a minister, he does not need to make the same effort as [Julien] or to harbour the same feelings: neither the sprung tension of will not the ardour of envy, hatred, and defiance. Hence he is without meaning, one ought even to say without character; for it was the difficulties of the struggle and the distance from his goal, together with his ambition, which constituted the character of Julien. Julien is always doing things, Fabrice is almost passive. ⟨. . .⟩ Finally, just as everything is less brightly coloured, less sharply defined, in *The Charterhouse* than in *The Red and the Black,* so the dénouement is greyer and flatter. One hastens to add, however, that it is also truer to life and more satisfying to our instinct for logic. In *The Red and the Black* everyone lost their wits, while in *The Charterhouse* everyone becomes resigned. ⟨. . .⟩ This dénouement, at least, in *The Charterhouse* is fully realist. It seems to be saying: all this enthusiasm, these great hopes, this passion for greatness, this Napoleonic spirit, where—after the great crisis and upheaval that has taken place in Europe—will they all soon lead? To resignation, to the tranquillity to be found in the monotony and selfishness of the bourgeois way of life. This story begins with young Fabrice's escapades at Waterloo and ends in the precautions and discretions of Monseigneur Fabrice del Dongo and Mme Clélia Crescenzi's well-regulated adultery. And so it goes in all our lives: we all start out with our own escapades at Waterloo, and we all have our equivalent of a bishopric in Parma to see us through until, at the end, we each of us make a 'charterhouse' for ourselves, in which to see out our days in silence and in solitude.

—Emile Faguet, "Stendhal," *Revue des Deux Mondes* 109 (1892). Reprinted in *Stendhal,* ed. Robert Pearson (London: Longman, 1994): pp. 52–53.

ROMANTICISM OF STENDHAL'S HEROES

[George Lukács (1885–1971), an influential Marxist theorist and literary critic, is the author of *The Theory of the Novel, Goethe and his Age,* and *Studies in European Realism,* from which the following passages are extracted. He discusses the way Stendhal's heroes remain uncorrupted by their participation in the "game" of capitalistic careerism, a trend that speaks to the presence of a strain of romanticism among Stendhal's values.]

What is at issue here is the central problem of the nineteenth-century world-view and style: the attitude to romanticism. No great writer living after the French revolution could avoid this issue. ⟨. . .⟩ The basic problem in dealing with this issue was that romanticism was by no means a purely literary trend; it was the expression of a deep and spontaneous revolt against rapidly developing capitalism, although, naturally in very contradictory forms. The extreme romanticists soon turned into feudalist reactionaries and obscurantists. But the background of the whole movement is nevertheless a spontaneous revolt against capitalism. All this provided a strange dilemma for the great writers of the age, who, while they were unable to rise above the *bourgeois* horizon, yet strove to create a world-picture that would be both comprehensive and real. They could not be romanticists in the strict sense of the word; had they been that, they could not have understood and followed the forward movement of their age. On the other hand they could not disregard the criticism levelled by the romanticists at capitalism and capitalist culture, without exposing themselves to the danger of becoming blind extollers of *bourgeois* society, and apologists of capitalism. They therefore had to attempt to overcome romanticism (in the Hegelian sense), i.e. to fight against it, preserve it and raise it to a higher level all at the same time. ⟨. . .⟩

⟨. . .⟩ What Balzac painted ⟨. . .⟩ is how the rise of capitalism to the undisputed economic domination of society carries the human and moral degradation and debasement of men into the innermost depths of their hearts.

Stendhal's composition is quite different. As a great realist, he of course sees all the essential phenomena of his time no less clearly than Balzac. ⟨. . .⟩ And as the great realist that he is, he allows his hero to take part in the game of corruption and careerism, to wade through all the filth of growing capitalism, to learn, and apply, sometimes even skilfully, the rules of the game as expounded by Mosca and Vautrin. But it is interesting to note that none of his principal characters is at heart sullied or corrupted by this participation in the "game." A pure and passionate ardour, an inexorable search for truth preserves from contamination the souls of these men as they wade through the mire, and helps them to shake off the dirt at the end of their career (but still in the prime of their youth), although it is true that by so doing they cease to be participants in the life of their time and withdraw from it in one way or another.

This is the deeply romantic element in the world-view of Stendhal the enlightened atheist and bitter opponent of romanticism. (The term 'romanticism' is of course used here in the widest, least dogmatic sense). It is in the last instance due to Stendhal's refusal to accept the fact that the heroic period of the *bourgeoisie* was ended and that the 'antediluvian colossi'—to us a Marxian phrase—had perished for ever. Every slightest trace of such heroic trends as he can find in the present (although mostly only in his own heroic, uncompromising soul) he exaggerates into proud reality and contrasts it satirico-elegiacally with the wretched dishonesty of his time.

—George Lukács, *Studies in European Realism*, trans. Edith Bone (London: Hillway Publishing Co., 1950): pp. 67–68, 80–81.

[Jean-Pierre Richard, a phenomenological critic in the line of Georges Poulet, has written *Littérature et sensation* and *Poesie et profondeur*. His remarks in the following passage focus on the significance of the privileged moment as the standard by which Stendhal's heroes tend to measure and judge their experiences.]

The Stendhalian hero faces the universe as unequipped and unprejudiced as the first man on the morning of Creation. Stendhal inherits from his eighteenth-century forbears the image of a hero naked and pure whom experience alone will gradually teach. Julien at the seminary, Fabrice at Waterloo, are both *ingénus,* worthy sons of Voltaire's Huron or of Montesquieu's Persian, formed by their own sensations, and led by them to the knowledge of things and to the awareness of themselves. However—and this is what makes them radically different from their elders—they are not content to wait passively for experience to come; they go out to meet it, and if need be even provoke it. A product of the Napoleonic era and a disciple of Maine de Biran, Stendhal was schooled in the virtues of activity and effort. Life looms before his heroes like a vast jungle of the senses, through which they will have to hack the most savory path they can. For them, happiness is not something to be awaited, as in the epicureanism of old; it is something to be pursued, to be forced. Sensation is a prey, at once the gift of chance and the reward of courage. The *chasse au bonheur* might then culminate in the triumph of one or two perfect moments, whose emotional content is enough to sum up and justify a lifetime.

Stendhal had known such moments. Very few of them, to be sure; but enough so that around them, as though around a few isolated peaks, the whole landscape of his life was ordered and arranged. ⟨. . .⟩ every lover of Stendhal knows and treasures these precious moments when chance managed to fulfill the needs of the soul to exact measure. Stendhal's own devotion to these moments is unflagging, and to the last he strives to preserve the trace of them within himself.

But it was precisely one of the great Stendhalian paradoxes, that a being so passionately dedicated to the pursuit of happiness should, in the end, confess how nearly powerless he was to describe for himself the various nuances of that happiness, and even to keep in focus his mental image of it. One can live or relive happiness, one cannot recount it; the very violence of its rapture prevents it from being examined or known. "There is one part of the sky we cannot see," writes Stendhal, "because it is too near the sun." All the more reason for our being unable to gaze at the sun itself. In a word, happiness, "the perfect happiness that a sensitive soul experiences with insatiable delight to the point of annihilation and madness," is a blinding ecstasy. When the blissful moment is past, when the sensitive soul returns from its trance to itself, it finds that it can only imperfectly recall that state of ecstasy in which it had immersed itself.

Such confusion, however, cannot satisfy Stendhal. To gratify his soul, the quest for happiness must not exclude the knowledge of happiness. Thus he will attempt to recall those seemingly lost moments, and to reclaim from indistinctness those overly powerful joys, those overly vague sensations. Stendhal's experience begins with passion, but his most lucid venture lies in circumscribing this passion, in knowing it fully, and in establishing between these burning moments of his life a continuity of feeling that poses no threat to his consciousness. ⟨. . .⟩

—Jean-Pierre Richard, *Littérature et sensation* (Paris: Editions du Seuil, 1954). Reprinted in *Stendhal: A Collection of Critical Essays,* ed. Victor Brombert (Englewood Cliffs, N.J.: Prentice-Hall, 1962): pp. 127–129.

⊛

Fabrizio's Transformation in Prison

[This excerpt from *Stendhal: Notes on a Novelist* centers on Fabrizio's transformation during his time in the Farnese Tower, from which he emerges a free artist of the emotions according to Robert M. Adams, who goes on to tease out some of the ironies attendant upon the change.]

Fabrizio del Dongo also comes in prison to know the self, the love, and full expression which society has done its utmost to deny him. There is an old Fabrizio to be buried here; the lover of Marietta and

Fausta, the handsome young man with an English horse, a carriage, a charming apartment, a half-dozen mistresses and an acute case of persistent boredom. But Fabrizio's dungeon is not only a place of burial, it is a two-hundred-and-thirty-foot erection, a cavern poised atop a tower. It serves Fabrizio as a pinnacle for emotional flight, a seedbed for the generation of his sensibility, a summit of power and happiness, a refuge from and a fulfillment of passion. Within the prison, which is his new and deepened self-consciousness, is accomplished mysteriously the crystallization of his soul and his love; within the prison he becomes an artist, a poet not merely in words but in feelings. The triple knot of Stendhalian sentiment, erotic, Narcissistic, and creative, is tightly tied in the depths of the dungeon and in the isolation of the lofty tower. As a result, Fabrizio becomes more whole and secure of feeling than ever before. ⟨. . .⟩ His piety, his ambition, and his love are combined, under the impulse of a new artistic unscrupulousness, to give him the vocation of a popular preacher; and the vehemence with which he publicly implores mercy of his mistress gains him credit with the unthinking for the utmost sanctity, just as his ambition is best served by the wearing of a shabby black coat. By the inversion of art he has been made, in Donne's phrase, "one of all."

Undoubtedly there lurks in this solution or resolution, a germ of the exquisite Stendhalian irony. The arrangement with Clélia, which hides just around the corner, has sardonic overtones which can scarcely be tied down to one circumstance. Having sworn before the Virgin that she will never see Fabrizio again, Clélia delicately conducts her affair with him in the dark. Touches like these fall just short of burlesque; and Fabrizio's whole church-career is not hard to see as a triumph of that legerdemain which amounts to rendering black white, white black, and black-and-white invisible. His crimes, if one wanted to spell them out sobersides, would be almost as many as those of Gina herself. But crimes are not all and equally crimes, for Stendhal; in the circumstances of a corrupt society, when performed with energy and without "lowness," when they are "interesting" and "passionate." . . . In the specific circumstance of Fabrizio, there is an element of seriousness in the observation that, where the business of society is to misuse language in its interests, the revenge of the artist is to make his own special perversions of speech in his own interests. The phrasing should not, ultimately, be cast in such vindictive terms, though vindictiveness is one element of the total reaction. The artist creates a refuge from society, he also does pleasure to society; and at the same time he sets it at secret defiance. This triple quality of the artistic response is, I think, a distinguishing and triumphant quality of the artistic subversion which Stendhal brilliantly exemplifies, and which he learned or at least developed during the years of his delinquency with that most disreputable of bad little girls, Angelina Pietragrua.

—Robert M. Adams, *Stendhal: Notes on a Novelist* (New York: Funk and Wagnalls, 1959): pp. 96–98.

⊗

THEME OF IMPRISONMENT

[Jean Starobinski has taught at Johns Hopkins and at the University of Geneva in Switzerland. He authored *History of Medicine, Blessings in Disguise or The Morality of Evil,* and *The Invention of Liberty, 1700–1789,* as well as *L'Oeil vivant,* from which the following remarks are drawn. He speculates here on connections between the theme of imprisonment in Stendhal's oeuvre and some of Stendhal's personal insecurities.]

In the case of Stendhal, the theme of confinement must be underlined. A name, a body, a social status, all are prisons. But their doors are not so well locked that the dream of escape is impossible. Of course, one takes leave of one's name more easily than of one's body, and a pseudonym is a substitute for the desired metamorphosis. (This impatience with having to tolerate one's body can be found in almost every writer who has had recourse to a pseudonym. However different, Voltaire and Kierkegaard share a certain anxious attention to their bodies and their ailments. In this sense pseudonymity represents a manifestation of hypochondria.)

In order to express this imprisonment, the metaphor of the cell naturally appears. One sees chains, thick walls, high well-guarded towers. These images stubbornly recur in Stendhal's works. The heroes who are imprisoned and who escape—Julien at the seminary, Fabrice in the Farnese tower, Hélène Campireale in the convent,

Lamiel at the Hautemares—seem each time to recreate an archetypal situation. The theme of *amour-passion* is curiously involved. Imprisonment corresponds to the birth of the highest form of love, which derives its power from its impossibility. Desire, then, implies distance and insurmountable separation. Octave, confined within the fatality of his impotence, loves Armance all the more ardently in that he can not abolish the impediment that keeps him from her. Octave, however, is loved in return, just as all the imprisoned heroes are loved in return in spite of the locks, or perhaps because of them. Extreme unhappiness thus meets extreme happiness. It is in this that one clearly sees the power of compensation that pervades Stendhal's fiction. If society avenges itself on the exceptional individual by imprisoning him, from his very high tower he can avenge himself on society by transforming his solitude into a contemptuous and hopeless happiness. The motif of high places, stressed by Proust as a fundamental theme in Stendhal, merges with the theme of confinement. These glorious prisoners need but one long look to dominate the world. In these heroes, who are visited by love in prison, one must recognize (among other things) the figurative transposition of Stendhal's secret desire—to be loved in spite of his ugliness, in spite of—the prison that his body and age are for him, to love and be loved from afar through the power of a glance. Destruction does not threaten this love, either because it can never be consummated in possession and marriage and is consequently never exposed to destruction, or because even if consummated it always remains furtive and clandestine, thus lightening in an extraordinary way the importance of the body.

> —Jean Starobinski, *L'Oeil vivant* (Paris: Gallimard, 1961). Reprinted in *Stendhal: A Collection of Critical Essays,* ed. Victor Brombert (Englewood Cliffs, N.J.: Prentice-Hall, 1962): pp. 119–120.

❀

Unity of Stendhal's Oeuvre

[Gérard Genette, an important Structuralist critic and theorist, has written *The Aesthetic Relation, Fiction and Diction,* and *Figures of Literary Discourse,* from which the following extract is drawn. According to Genette, Stendhal's oeuvre manifests a thematic unity, rather than a social or temporal cohesion, and thus lends itself to a "paradigmatic reading."]

⟨. . .⟩ There is no unity of place or time, no recurrence of characters, no trace of that wish to compete with the legal status by creating an autonomous, complete, and coherent society; a few erratic novels, devoid of any linking principle, scattered throughout a heterogeneous oeuvre, of which they are far from constituting the main body, at least in quantity: like Rousseau, or Barrès, or Gide, Stendhal is quite obviously an impure novelist. For all that, though, the unity of Stendhalian fiction is unquestionable, but it is not one of cohesion, still less of continuity. It stems entirely from a sort of strictly thematic constancy: a unity of repetition and variation, which relates, rather than links, these novels to one another.

Gilbert Durand has brought out the most important of these recurrent themes. The solitude of the hero and the reinforcement of his destiny by the duplication (or uncertainty) of his birth and oracular overdetermination; testing trials and temptations; feminine duality and symbolic opposition between the two types of the Amazon (or "sublime whore"—Mathilde, Vanina, Mina de Vanghel, Mme de Hocquincourt, la Sanseverina) and the tender woman, guardian of the heart's secrets (Mme de Rênal, Mme de Chasteller, Clélia Conti); the conversion of the hero and the passage from the epic register to that of tender intimacy (symbolized at least twice, in *Le Rouge et le noir* and the *Chartreuse,* by the paradoxical motif of the happy prison), which defines precisely the *moment* of Stendhalian fiction: even, it seems to me, contrary to the view expressed by Durand, in the first part of *Leuwen,* where we see a hero originally convinced, like Fabrizio, of being incapable of love, and forewarned against this feeling by political prejudice ⟨. . .⟩ discover "that he has a heart" and become converted to his passion.

This fundamental theme of the *Rücksicht,* of the abandonment to female tenderness as a return to the mother, reinforced still more by the typically maternal appearance and function of the triumphant heroine (including Clélia, who is more maternal, despite her age and kinship, than the conquering Sanseverina), lies therefore at the basis of what is most essential in Stendhal's fictional creation, which scarcely alters, from one work to another, except in rhythm and tonality. The reader is thus led to make endless comparisons between situations, characters, feelings, actions, instinctively bringing out correspondences by superimposition and change of perspective. A network of interferences is thus set up between Julien, Fabrizio, and Lucien, between Mathilde and Gina, Mme de Rênal, Mme de Chasteller, and Clélia, between François Leuwen, M. de la Môle, and Conte Mosca, Chélan and Blanès, Sansfin and Du Poirier, Frilair and Rassi, the suspect paternities of Julien and Fabrizio, their common devotion to Napoleon, between the Farnese tower and Besançon prison, between the seminary, the garrison at Nancy, and the battle-field of Waterloo, etc. More than any other, no doubt, Stendhal's *oeuvre* invites a *paradigmatic* reading, in which the consideration of narrative links fades before the evidence of relations of homology: a harmonic, or vertical, reading, then, a reading on two or several registers, for the reader for whom the true text begins with the duplication of the text.

—Gérard Genette, Figures of Literary Discourse, trans. Alan Sheridan (New York: Columbia University Press, 1982): pp. 167–168.

☙

Waterloo Episode

[In this passage from *Stendhal: Fiction and the Themes of Freedom,* Victor Brombert reads the Waterloo episode as a mock-heroic parody in which the epic commonplaces that inform Fabrizio's visions of military grandeur are satirized in order to bring out his indomitably "poetic" nature.]

The most striking illustration of Stendhalian ambiguities in *La Chartreuse* is the famous Waterloo episode. Stendhal has been praised for his "realistic" account, for having been the first writer to systematically describe a battle from the point of view of a single consciousness, through the eyes of a single character utterly puzzled by what goes on, and who, instead of dominating the historic event with the perspective and omniscience of a historian, is only able to witness movement and confusion. ⟨. . .⟩ With Fabrice at Waterloo, we are far indeed from the Homeric or Virgilian epic slaughters where every participant, weapon, skirmish, and wound is catalogued and described by the poet-strategist.

But if the epic description is debunked by implication, so is the epic hero. Fabrice, in love with the sound of cannons, thirsts for noble sensations. A romantic Candide, he would like to gallop after every one of Napoleon's marshals. He is, in fact, a heroic parasite, inexperienced and totally superfluous on the field of battle. The author treats him with deliberate irony. ⟨. . .⟩ We are invited to laugh at Fabrice's naïveté, his clumsiness, his illusions, and at the deflation of his dreams of heroic comradeship. He discovers that war resembles neither Ariosto's poem nor the proclamations of the Emperor. As the author leads Fabrice from surprise to surprise, from blunder to blunder, from one humiliating experience to another, it becomes quite evident that what these pages propose is not at all a "realistic" account, but a mock-heroic episode, a parody of epic attitudes and conventions.

Conventional epic elements are in fact repeatedly stressed, but in order, it would seem, to attract attention to obvious discrepancies. A grand spectacle, a hero traveling far from his home country and involved in a series of actions filled with obstacles and dangers, enormous crowds, mysterious omens and predictions, battles pitting entire nations against each other, a collective awareness that the future of an entire continent is at stake—nothing seems to be missing. Yet it is all strangely unauthentic, like a literary game. Fabrice, like Don Quixote, has read too many books. His overexcited imagination attempts to impose the patterns of heroic romance on a banal and recalcitrant reality. ⟨. . .⟩

—Victor Brombert, *Stendhal: Fiction and the Themes of Freedom* (New York: Random House, 1968): pp. 155–156, 158.

REPRESENTATION OF HAPPINESS

[Leo Bersani has taught at Rutgers University and is currently on the faculty at the University of California at Berkeley. He is the author of *Baudelaire and Freud, Caravaggio's Secrets,* and *Balzac to Beckett: Center and Circumference in French Fiction,* from which the following extract is drawn. Bersani examines the risks involved in representing happiness in the novel, as well as the ways in which conflicts born of social tensions help Stendhal to manage such risks without corrupting the integrity of his vision.]

⟨. . .⟩ In other words, the love between Fabrice and Clélia contains almost no possibilities for dramatic conflict, variety, or progress; indeed, its very ideality would seem to depend on a spiritual immobility. It perhaps also realizes, more generally, a wish for a peaceful, somewhat monotonous harmony with the world, which is to say that it overcomes the divisions, the differentiations which create pain but which are also the inspirations of language and of novelistic invention.

Stendhal uses the painful divisions and antagonisms of life to save both his work and himself from the infantile fantasy which is his hero's dangerous paradise. ⟨. . .⟩ Imprisonment comes to Fabrice as a relief, and we find ourselves willing to believe that the most important problem in the hero's life is how to saw away part of the shutter and make an alphabet with which to send messages to Clélia. But the atmosphere of play is, of course, somewhat deceptive; it is transformed into one of urgent vigilance by the fact that Fabrice's life is in danger as long as he stays in prison. Fabrice is indifferent to this danger, but the lovers' prison games would have much less interest for *us* if their inventiveness were not a question of life and death. The society excluded by Fabrice's cell continues to provide threats which inspire the activities of prison life. And happiness "exploits" society in this way throughout the novel. The substance, the matter of fiction is provided by the enemy of its highest pleasures: Parma. The space of the novel is filled with political detail which suffocates The Happy Few but at the same time creates the tension, the drama, the life that keep the story moving. It interrupts a happiness about which, finally, there is very little to *say*. ⟨. . .⟩ Stendhal's tireless attention to a society which destroys the paradise of play also creates the verbal environment in which happiness—essentially nonverbal and unnovelistic—can be evoked as that which is missing.

Missing, and yet, by a curious final twist, referred to by this society just as surely as this type of social image is implicit in the Stendhalian image of happiness. The hostile father and the hostile society are necessary both to bring the hero into the world and to vindicate his retreat from the world. Politics and happiness as I have defined them are the two magnetic poles of Stendhal's fiction. They provide what might be called the structural differentiation of a single fantasy of threatened and threatening unity between the self and the world. The court at Parma is the "natural" partner of the idyll in the Farnese tower, the ideally divisive complement to an ideally harmonious union. The type of society we find in *La Chartreuse* is implied by images of happiness which are consistently images of flight and seclusion. The paradise of the Stendhalian hero is a kind of death-in-life, and the deepest needs of Fabrice and Julien are actually best served by the society they live in. What other alternative than a retreat to the peace and safe isolation of childhood is left to them by this cruel, agitated world of men? Society saves the Stendhalian vision of happiness from the self-containment and purposelessness of mere being, but its very hostility also reinforces the hero's choices, justifies his joyful self-imprisonments.

> —Leo Bersani, *Balzac to Beckett: Center and Circumference in French Fiction* (New York: Oxford University Press, 1970): pp. 120–121.

☙

HISTORY AND ROMANCE

> [In this excerpt from *Stendhal,* Michael Wood discusses the way in which the political and historical elements of *The Charterhouse of Parma* combine to inform its status as "a romance."]

But surely *La Chartreuse de Parme* is a contemporary political novel: Stendhal took the trouble to modernize his old chronicle. How then can it be a romance, in any sense? In fact, the mere possibility of a modernization simply continues and strengthens the argument. Julien Sorel was not able to translate over a period of less than twenty years, the Napoleonic model ran him into all kinds of difficulties in the Restoration. Here Stendhal shifts a whole story, with pope, cardinals and a dazzling courtesan, two hundred years at a blow, and without any effort. For Rome read Parma, for pope read prince, for cardinal read minister. Only

Gina is a sparkling anachronism, a restless, brilliant, woman from another age. There are changes to be made, of course. The violent vendettas of the Renaissance have given way to the small politics of the Congress of Vienna. The prince of Parma, far from assassinating his enemies wholesale, has once had two liberals hanged, and now goes in mortal fear for his life—Mosca's chief credit with his sovereign being his ability to make the prince's panic look less emasculating than it is. It is Mosca who suggests they look under the bed at night and even in the cases of the bass fiddles. But the general result of the switch from the sixteenth century is not to bring things up to date but to suggest that nothing has changed. Fabrice on his way back from Waterloo is insulted, he thinks, in a café, and promptly forgets all the modern etiquette he has learned. He doesn't consider a duel, he draws his dagger and leaps on his enemy—'Fabrice's first movement was right out of the sixteenth century'.

Italy has progressed only towards pettiness. Otherwise it is the same backward, quarrelling, ungovernable place it always was. Stendhal's portrait is affectionate, but not complimentary.

His novel becomes timeless, then, as ultimately all historical novels are. It is released from contemporary contingencies, a romance. But it is tired romance, an ironic idyll, the world it offers is not better or brighter than the real one, it is simply safer, a world with familiar pitfalls and antagonists, a shelter from the new and unexpected. The retreat is not into fantasy but into chess or mathematics, into a place where the rules of the game are known and if you can keep your scruples quiet—for why should you air them, if they can have no possible effect—the game can be fun. 'Games, in Stendhal', as Blackmur remarkably said, 'are how you handle the incomprehensible.'

—Michael Wood, *Stendhal* (Ithaca: Cornell University Press, 1971): pp. 171–172.

[Alison Finch has lectured at Churchill College of Cambridge University and is currently a Reader in French at Merton College, Oxford University. She is the author of *Women's Writing in Nineteenth-Century France* and *Stendhal:* La Chartreuse de Parme, from which the following comments are drawn. She offers a summary analysis of the representation of love in the novel, focusing first on the interlocking love-triangles at the heart of the novel and then moving on to examine Stendhal's sophisticated treatment of the theme of incest.]

La Chartreuse shows, however, important new developments in Stendhal's portrayal of love: for instance, his detailed creation of *two* couples—Mosca and Gina, Fabrice and Clélia—with the cross-relationship Gina-Fabrice. These allow most interesting comparisons between unconscious love, reflective love, guilty love, and rapidly acknowledged desires. Mosca's love for Gina is more thoughtful than Fabrice's for Clélia; Gina's for Mosca—and even for Fabrice—freer of self-reproach than Clélia's.

Certain obstacles to love again differ in their nature from those of previous novels. Stendhal's portrait of Leuwen *père* in *Lucien Leuwen* provides his closest and perhaps best analysis of both the comic and serious sides of family love. But *La Chartreuse* asks wide-ranging and disturbing questions about it: about how far, for instance, family love too may be intensified to a tragic degree by an alternation between frustration and tantalizing contacts. This is the case of Fabrice and his son; finally, the obstacles between them give Fabrice the idea of abducting Sandrino that serves as a climax to the novel: for his idea is called 'ce *malheureux caprice* de *tendresse*', and these three words sum up much of the atmosphere of *La Chartreuse.* Tantalizing contacts and difficulties also mark Gina's love for Fabrice, a love now created, now discouraged, now brought to a violent pitch at least in part by the fact that although not his blood-relation, she is of his family.

The theme of incest was a fashionable one in early nineteenth-century literature, exploited by, for instance, Shelley and Chateaubriand. Stendhal was, no doubt, also guided towards the theme by his own rewriting of the brutal and incestuous tale of the

Cenci in *Chroniques italiennes.* But Stendhal handles the 'suppositions' and the 'facts' of incest very differently from his contemporaries: less sentimentally and sensationally, more humanely. He neither overemphasizes the sexuality of Gina's love for Fabrice nor underplays its parental aspects. Her love starts as one shared with her first husband in a childless marriage, and at other points in the novel her complaints of neglect, or fears for Fabrice's safety, could just as easily be maternal as erotic. Even the later headstrong interference between Fabrice and Clélia has as many antecedents in the fathers of Molière's plays as in the thwarted heroines of Racine's. Her own awareness of the eroticism—or what Stendhal suggests of this awareness—fluctuates greatly, and Stendhal, through carefully chosen under-statements or modest periphrases, often leaves a margin of doubt as to its nature. ⟨. . .⟩

It is because Gina's jealousy wavers between the sexually legitimate and the taboo that it finally attains such force. Critics have noticed, of course, that Gina changes in the course of the novel—that her drive to act becomes less often bravery than imprudence, and that her resolute quality can become an unrelenting vindictiveness; and some have stated that this is the 'end result' of the 'impetuous personality'—that Gina's very involvement with the present moment must lead to a blind wilfulness. However, on almost all those occasions when Gina acts foolishly, dangerously, or cruelly it is her love for Fabrice that propels her; and Stendhal further suggests the social dangers of incestuous love, and the tragic sides of its frustrations, by evoking the myth of Phaedra ⟨. . .⟩.

—Alison Finch, *Stendhal:* La Chartreuse de Parme (London: Edward Arnold, 1984): pp. 56–57.

⊗

SPEECHLESSNESS AND MYTH

[Roland Barthes (1915–1980) taught in Romania and Egypt and later in France at the Ecole Pratique des Hautes Etudes and the Collège de France. A highly influential critic, his works include *Writing Degree Zero, Mythologies, S/Z,* and

The Pleasure of the Text. Here Barthes describes how the novelistic conventions of *The Charterhouse of Parma* liberate Stendhal from the speechlessness that marks his Italian journals, a speechlessness, according to Barthes, that is always "generated by an excess of love: before Italy and Women, and Music," Stendhal is "ceaselessly interrupted in his locution."]

To keep to these Journals, which betoken a love of Italy but do not communicate it (at least, such is the judgment of my own reading), we are entitled to repeat mournfully (or tragically) that *one always fails in speaking of what one loves.* Yet, twenty years later, by a kind of after-the-fact which also constitutes part of the devious logic of love, Stendhal writes certain triumphant pages about Italy which, this time, fire up the reader (this reader—but I don't suppose I'm the only one) with that jubilation, with that *irradiation* which the private journals claimed but did not communicate. These admirable pages are the ones which form the beginning of *The Charterhouse of Parma.* Here there is a kind of miraculous harmony between "the mass of happiness and pleasure which explodes" in Milan with the arrival of the French and our own delight in reading: the effect described finally coincides with the effect produced. Why this reversal? Because Stendhal, shifting from the Journal to the Novel, from the Album to the Book (to adopt one of Mallarmé's distinctions), has abandoned sensation, a vivid but inconstruable fragment, to undertake that great mediating form which is Narrative, or better still Myth. What is required to make a Myth? We must have the action of two forces: first of all, a hero, a great liberating figure: this is Bonaparte, who enters Milan, penetrates Italy, as Stendhal did, more humbly, from the Saint-Bernard pass; then an opposition, an antithesis—a paradigm, in short—which stages the combat of Good and Evil and thereby produces what is lacking in the Album and belongs to the Book, i.e., a meaning: on one side, in these first pages of *The Charterhouse,* boredom, wealth, avarice, Austria, the Police, Ascanio, Grianta; on the other, intoxication, heroism, poverty, the Republic, Fabrizio, Milan; and above all, on the one side, the Father; on the other, Women. By abandoning himself to the Myth, by entrusting himself to the Book, Stendhal gloriously regains what he had somehow failed to achieve in his albums: the expression of an effect. This effect—the Italian effect—finally has a name, which is no longer the platitudinous one of Beauty: it is festivity. Italy is a feast, that is what is ultimately conveyed by the Milanese preamble of *The Charterhouse*, which Stendhal was quite right to retain, despite Balzac's reservations: festivity, i.e., the very transcendence of egotism.

In short, what has happened—what has transpired—between the travel journals and *The Charterhouse*, is writing. Writing—which annuals the sterile immobility of the amorous image-repertoire and gives its adventure a symbolic generality. When he was young, in the days of *Rome, Naples, Florence*, Stendhal could write: "...when I tell lies, I am like M. de Goury, I am bored"; he did not yet know that there existed a lie, the lie of novels, which would be—miraculously—both the detour of truth and the finally triumphant expression of his Italian passion.

—Roland Barthes, *The Rustle of Language,* trans. Richard Howard (Oxford: Basil Blackwell, 1986): pp. 304–305.

ELLIPSIS IN THE NOVEL

[A Pulitzer Prize–winning poet and distinguished translator, Richard Howard teaches comparative literature at the University of Cincinnati. His translation of *The Charterhouse of Parma* was published in 1999 in the Modern Library series, and the following remarks are drawn from his "Afterword" to that edition. Howard meditates here on the elliptical quality the novel manifests, compiling a miniature index of the book's unstable categories and patterns of evasion, and concludes with his own provocatively elliptical suggestion that the novel has neither a hero nor a heroine.]

Nothing fixed. "The man," Nietzsche said, "was a human question-mark." And he suggested the tone, the reason for it and the consequence of it: "Objection, evasion, joyous distrust, and love of irony are signs of health; everything absolute belongs to pathology."

Consider Gina's two husbands: Count Pietranera, who prefers living in poverty to political compromise, and Count Mosca, for whom politics is a game and any conviction a liability. All political life is marked by incoherence. As Professor Talbot puts it, conservatives become liberals when out of power, and liberals become conservatives when in power.

Consider, again, Fabrizio's roles; in the first third of the novel he claims to be a barometer merchant, a captain of the Fourth Regiment of hussars, a young bourgeois in love with that captain's wife, Teulier, Boulot, Cavi, Ascanio Pietranera, and an unnamed peasant. Further, he will assume a disguise to visit Marietta's apartment, will use Giletti's name and passport to go through customs, assume another disguise as a rich country bourgeois; then claim to be Ludovic's brother, then Joseph Bossi, a theology student. With Fausta, he passes himself off as the valet of an English lord; in the duel with Count M—— he calls himself Bombace. And under all this, his conviction that he is a del Dongo. Nor is he even that—he is the son of a French lieutenant named Robert billeted in the del Dongo palace in Milan during the French occupation; therefore Gina is not his aunt, though on one occasion early in the novel she passes Fabrizio off as her *son!* . . . Evading the love of a woman he believes to be his aunt, Fabrizio ends in a prison originally built to house a crown prince guilty of incest.

Nothing fixed: Fabrizio is not a soldier, though he may have fought at Waterloo; not for a moment do we believe he is a cleric, though he is made archbishop of Parma; he is pure becoming, and the language he uses must show him to us in that form, that formlessness. . . .

Translate this book to exorcise the fetishism of the Work conceived as an hermetic object, finished, absolute . . . (Beyle, the anti-Flaubert). Nothing in this novel, "complete" though it may be, is quite closed over itself, autonomous in its genesis, and its signification. Hence Balzac's suggestion to erase Parma altogether and call the book something like "Adventures of a typical Italian youth. . . ." Remember that the novel opens as the story of the Duchess Sanseverina. And ends with the "throttled" disappearance (Beyle's phrase, in protest against the publisher's insistence that the book fit in two volumes) of everyone but Mosca, "immensely rich." Such vacillation is never satisfied. More than *Vanity Fair,* this is a Novel Without a Hero, without a Heroine, a novel without. . . .

—Richard Howard, "Afterword," *The Charterhouse of Parma* (New York: Random House, 1999): pp. 504–505.

[In this excerpt from *How to Read and Why,* Harold Bloom links *The Charterhouse of Parma* to works by Shakespeare, Cervantes, and Lord Byron, analyzing Stendhal's unique engagement with the reader in relation to the novel's portrayal of the vanity inherent in romantic love.]

Stendhal has learned from Shakespeare (and from his own romantic disasters) the arbitrariness of all grand passions, and from Cervantes he has learned that passion, even when it kills, is a mode of play. All is irony, unless you happen to be one of the four lovers caught inside this chess game. The play, as Balzac saw, was of private passions; the age of Napoleon was over. We are postchivalric, and what matters are the four lovers. Romance is everything, once Wellington has triumphed. Julien Sorel, in *The Red and the Black,* pursues his suicidal and more or less heroic erotic career as a Napoleonic clone bound to undergo a *sparagmos* in the Restoration. But post-Congress-of-Vienna Parma is a sublime madness, where everything goes, and nothing works for long, except the sadly noble survivor Mosca, who ends up rich but deprived of his Gina, who has lost her Fabrice, who is divested of his Clélia. [. . .]

Fabrice's affection for Gina, though intense, is limited; Romeo-like, he will fall in love with Clélia at first sight, and it will become, as in Shakespeare, a kind of love-death. He is never in love with his quasi-aunt, Gina, though he has more regard for her than for anyone else. The center of Stendhal's concern, and so the focus of the novel, is Gina's unrequited passion, since she is the most remarkable and achieved character in the novel. The *Charterhouse* ultimately matters because she does; no other figure in Stendhal is so vital and fascinating, or ultimately as Shakespearean and Cervantine. Gina is the glory of Stendhal's career as a writer. ⟨. . .⟩

Gina Pietranera, the Duchess Sanseverina, has giant flaws in her personality and moral character, but they serve only to enhance her interest for us. Rarely prudent, caught up by the possibilities of the moment, Gina captivates (and alarms) us by her passionate (and destructive) sincerity. As a High Romantic, mad about women, Stendhal has earned the approbation of Simone de Beauvoir, who in *The Second Sex* praised him as "a man who lives among women of flesh and blood." Gina is the most persuasive representation of those women that Stendhal achieved.

Stendhal, though always praised as a psychologist of heterosexual love, seems to me more a metaphysician in search of the barely conscious truth of desire. Vanity, he finds, is at the center of passionate love, or rather, if you fall in love, then everything in your condition that is not pathology is vanity. The reader, particularly if she is in love, may be unsettled by Stendhal, yet also enlightened.

The pleasures of *The Charterhouse of Parma,* as of *The Red and the Black,* are not those of sustained rapture. Stendhal writes as he is inspired, but he doesn't want to inspire us. Rather, he wishes us to learn to see erotic coldness as vanity, and passion as vanity raised to madness. His men and women are not Quixotic but Napoleonic, and even their most authentic attachments, however heroic, are self-destructive. Byron, though Stendhal might have wished otherwise, is closer to Stendhal than Shakespeare was; the *Charterhouse* attempts to render Fabrice and Clélia into Romeo and Juliet, but sometimes they seem more like lovers in *Don Juan.* ⟨. . .⟩

"A skeptic who believed in love"; is Valéry's summary of Stendhal accurate for the *Charterhouse*? I doubt that the mature Shakespeare "believed in love," and I am not at all certain about Stendhal.

Valéry though also noted Stendhal's shrewd drawing of the reader into complicity, which I suspect Stendhal had learned from Cervantes. Stendhal's true belief (as Valéry also intimates) was in the natural self, both his own and the reader's. Sometimes the reader may feel that Stendhal flatters her egotism (and his own), but he means well by her. To be made one of his "happy few" is a large benefit, because greater self-clarification will come from it. ⟨. . .⟩

—Harold Bloom, *How to Read and Why* (New York: Scribner, 2000): pp. 152–155.

Works by Stendhal

Lives of Haydn, Mozart, and Metastasio. 1814.

History of Painting in Italy. 1817.

Rome, Naples, and Florence in 1817. 1817.

On Love. 1822.

Racine and Shakespeare. 1823.

Life of Rossini. 1824.

Armance. 1827.

A Roman Journal. 1829.

The Red and the Black. 1830.

Memoirs of a Tourist. 1838.

The Charterhouse of Parma. 1839.

A Life of Napoleon. 1876.

Journal of Stendhal. 1888.

Lamiel. 1889.

The Life of Henri Brulard. 1890.

Memoirs of an Egotist. 1892.

Lucien Leuwen. 1894.

Works about
Stendhal

Adams, Robert M. *Stendhal: Notes on a Novelist.* New York: Noonday Press, 1959.

Alter, Robert, and Carol Cosman. *A Lion for Love: A Critical Biography of Stendhal.* New York: Basic, 1979.

Amoss, Benjamin McRae. *Time and Narrative in Stendhal.* Athens, Georigia: University of Georgia Press, 1992.

Auerbach, Erich. "In the Hôtel de la Mole." In *Mimesis: The Representation of Reality in Western Literature,* trans. Willard Trask. Princeton: Princeton University Press, 1953.

Barthes, Roland. "One Always Fails in Speaking of What One Loves." In *The Rustle of Language,* trans. Richard Howard. Oxford: Basil Blackwell, 1986.

Bersani, Leo. "Stendhalian Prisons and Salons." In *Balzac to Beckett: Center and Circumference in French Fiction.* New York: Oxford University Press, 1970.

Blin, Georges. *Stendhal et les problèmes du roman.* Paris: Corti, 1954.

———. *Stendhal et les problèmes du personnalité.* Paris: Corti, 1958.

Bloom, Harold, ed. *Stendhal's* The Red and the Black. New York: Chelsea House, 1988.

Brombert, Victor. *Stendhal et la voie oblique.* Paris: Presses Universitaires de France, 1954.

———. ed. *Stendhal: A Collection of Critical Essays.* Englewood Cliffs, New Jersey: Prentice-Hall, 1962.

———. *Stendhal: Fiction and the Themes of Freedom.* New York: Random House, 1968.

Brooks, Peter. "The Novel and the Guillotine, or Fathers and Sons in *Le Rouge et le Noir.*" In *Reading for the Plot: Design and Intention in Narrative.* New York: Knopf, 1984.

Del Litto, Victor. *La Vie intellectuelle de Stendhal.* Paris: Presses Universitaires de France, 1959.

Durand, Gilbert. *Le Décor mythique de la Chartreuse de Parme.* Paris: Corti, 1961.

Felman, Shoshana. *La Folie dans l'oeuvre Romanesque de Stendhal.* Paris: Corti, 1971.

Finch, Allison. *Stendhal:* La Chartreuse de Parme. London: Edward Arnold, 1984.

Fowlie, Wallace. *Stendhal.* London: Macmillan, 1969.

Genette, Gérard. "Stendhal." *Figures of Literary Discourse,* trans. Alan Sheridan. New York: Columbia University Press, 1982.

Gilman, Stephen. *The Tower as Emblem.* Frankfurt: Vittorio Klostermann, 1967.

Girard, René. "*The Red and the Black.*" In *Deceit, Desire, and the Novel,* trans. Yvonne Freccero. Baltimore: Johns Hopkins Press, 1965.

Golsan, Katherine. "History's Waterloo: Prediction in *La Chartreuse de Parme.*" *Nineteenth-Century French Studies* 24 (Spring–Summer 1996): 332–346

Haig, Stirling. *Stendhal:* The Red and the Black. Cambridge: Cambridge University Press, 1989.

———, and Dean de la Motte, eds. *Approaches to Teaching Stendhal's* The Red and the Black. New York: Modern Language Association of America, 1999.

Hemmings, F. W. J. *Stendhal: A Study of His Novels.* Oxford: Clarendon, 1964.

Howe, Irving. "Stendhal: The Politics of Survival." In *Politics and the Novel.* New York: Horizon Press, 1957.

Jameson, Maureen. "Mediation, Parasitism and Intertextuality in *La Chartreuse de Parme.*" *French Forum* 17 (September 1992): 261–279.

Jefferson, Ann. "Stendhal and the Uses of Reading: *Le Rouge et le noir.*" *French Studies* 37 (April 1983): 168–183.

———. *Reading Realism in Stendhal.* Cambridge: Cambridge University Press, 1988.

Krutch, Joseph Wood. "Stendhal." In *Five Masters: A Study in the Mutations of the Novel.* Bloomington: Indiana University Press, 1959.

Levin, Harry. "Stendhal." In *The Gates of Horn.* New York: Oxford University Press, 1963.

Lukács, George. "Balzac and Stendhal." In *Studies in European Realism,* trans. Edith Bone. London: Hillway Publishing Co., 1950.

Martineau, Henri. *L'Oeuvre de Stendhal: Histoire de ses livres et de sa pensée.* Paris: Albin Michel, 1951.

———. *Le Coeur de Stendhal.* 2 vols. Paris: Albin Michel, 1952–53.

Mauldon, Margaret. "Generic Survival: *Le Rouge et le Noir* and the Epistolary Tradition." *French Studies* 38 (October 1984): 414–422.

Miller, D. A. "Narrative 'Uncontrol' in Stendhal." In *Narrative and Its Discontents: Problems of Closure in the Traditional Novel.* Princeton: Princeton University Press, 1981.

Mossman, Carol A. *The Narrative Matrix: Stendhal's* Le Rouge et le noir. Lexington, Kentucky: French Forum Publishers, 1984.

O'Connor, Frank. "Stendhal: The Flight from Reality." In *The Mirror in the Roadway.* New York: Knopf, 1956.

Pearson, Roger, ed. *Stendhal:* The Red and the Black *and* The Charterhouse of Parma. London: Longman, 1994.

———. *Stendhal's Violin: A Novelist and His Reader.* Oxford: Clarendon Press, 1988.

Pollard, Patrick. "Color Symbolism in *Le Rouge et le noir.*" *Modern Language Review* 76(1981): 323–31.

Prendergast, Christopher. "Stendhal: The Ethics of Verisimilitude." In *The Order of Mimesis: Balzac, Stendhal, Nerval, Flaubert.* Cambridge: Cambridge University Press, 1986.

Prevost, Jean. *La Création chez Stendhal.* Paris: Mercure de France, 1951.

Proust, Marcel. "Notes sur Stendhal." In *Contre Saint-Beuve.* Paris: Gallimard, 1959.

Richard, Jean-Pierre. "Connaissance et tendresse chez Stendhal." In *Littérature et sensation.* Paris: Editions du Seuil, 1954.

Starobinski, Jean. "Stendhal pseudonyme." In *L'Oeil vivant.* Paris: Gallimard, 1961.

Strickland, Geoffrey. *Stendhal: The Education of a Novelist.* Cambridge: Cambridge University Press, 1974.

Talbot, Emile J. *Stendhal Revisited.* New York: Twayne Publishers, 1993.

Wood, Michael. *Stendhal.* Ithaca, New York: Cornell University Press, 1971.

Index of
Themes and Ideas